Peter M. Snaith

The
Street Chef

~ Making the World a Better Place to Eat ~

Outskirts Press, Inc.
Denver, Colorado

The opinions expressed in this manuscript are solely the opinions of the author and do not represent the opinions or thoughts of the publisher. The author represents and warrants that s/he either owns or has the legal right to publish all material in this book. If you believe this to be incorrect, contact the publisher through its website at www.outskirtspress.com.

The Street Chef
Making the World a Better Place to Eat
All Rights Reserved
Copyright © 2005 Peter M. Snaith

This book may not be reproduced, transmitted, or stored in whole or in part by any means, including graphic, electronic, or mechanical without the express written consent of the publisher except in the case of brief quotations embodied in critical articles and reviews.

Outskirts Press
http://www.outskirtspress.com

ISBN-10: 1-59800-111-6
ISBN-13: 978-1-59800-111-2

Library of Congress Control Number: 2005932030

Outskirts Press and the "OP" logo are trademarks belonging to
Outskirts Press, Inc.

Printed in the United States of America

Table of Contents

The Art of Cooking by Technique 1

The Street Chef's Seasoning Mixtures 11

Beef Brisket Rub 12
Creole Seafood Seasoning 12
Indian Seasoning 13
Jamaican Seasoning 13
Poultry Seasoning 14
Raz Al Hanout (Moroccan Spice) 14
Southwestern Seasoning 15
Steak Seasoning 15

The Art of Making Stocks 16

Vegetable Stock / Stock Basics 17
Veal Stock / Beef Stock 18
Chicken Stock 19
Shrimp Stock 20
Fish Stock 20

The Art of Making Sauces 21

Mother Sauces: 22
Béchamel 22
Velouté 22
Espagnole (Basic Brown Sauce) 23
Hollandaise 24
Vinaigrette 25

Vinaigrette Recipes 27

    Champagne Vinaigrette 28
    Rice Wine Vinaigrette 28

Sauce Recipes 29

    Alfredo Sauce 30
    Barbecue Sauce 31
    Barbecue Sauce Basics - Mustard Based 32
    Barbecue Sauce Basics - Tomato Based 33
    Barbecue Sauce Basics - Vinegar Based 34
    Blackberry Pan Sauce 34
    Brandy Veal Stock Reduction 35
    Chipotle Tomato Salsa 36
    Garlic and Mushroom Butter Cream Sauce 37
    Lemon Veal Glaze Sauce 38
    Lime Butter Sauce 39
    Mango Salsa 40
    Red Wine Pan Sauce 40
    Simple Tomato Sauce 41
    Spirit Pan Sauce 42
    Tomatillo Salsa 43
    Tomato Concasse Sauce 44
    Tomato Vodka Sauce 45
    Wild Mushroom Sauce 46

The Art of Making Soups 47

    Clarified Soups 48
    Meats in Soups 48
    Garnish for Soups 49

Soup Recipes 50

    Champagne Soup with Smoked Chicken 51
    Cream of Mushroom Soup 52
    Green Chili Soup 53
    Hearty Beer & Cheese Soup 54
    Roasted Acorn Squash Soup 55
    Roasted Chestnut Soup 56
    Roasted Corn and Chorizo Soup 57
    Roasted Corn Chowder 58
    Smoked Chicken Soup 59
    Tortilla Soup 60
    Tuscana Soup 61

Knife Skills 62

    Construction of the Knife 63
    Knife Production 64
    Purchasing a Knife 65
    Types of Knives and Their Uses 65
    Types of Edges 67
    Sharpening and Steeling 67
    Method for Using a Wet Stone 68
    Method for Using a Steel 68
    Holding the Knife 68
    Basic Culinary Cuts 68
    Other Knife Techniques 71

How to Choose a Steak 72

    Buying Steak 72
    Prepping the Steak 73
    Grilling Steak 74
    Pan-Seared and Oven-Roasted Steak 74
    Serving 74
    Choosing Other Cuts of Beef 75
    Basic Cuts of Lamb 75

Beef, Veal, and Pork Recipes 77

    Cajun Empanadas 78
    Carne Asada 80
    Hungarian Goulash 81
    Meatloaf for Sandwiches 82
    Mechado ala Marie - A Typical Filipino Dish 83
    Negimaki 84
    New Shepherds Pie 85
    Osso Bucco 86
    Pork Chops with Caramelized Onion Pan Gravy 87
    Sausages in Grape Sauce 88

Lamb Recipes 89

    Lamb Kabobs 90
    Merguez Kefta 91
    Rack of Lamb Stuffed with Brandy Macerated Apricots 92

The Art of Smoking 93

Smoking Recipes 95

Smoked Brisket 95
Smoked Chicken 96
Smoked Duck Breast 97
Smoked Pork Tacos 98
Smoked Stuffed Tomatoes 99
Southwestern Smoked Stuffed Tomatoes 100
Tea-Smoked Duck 102

How to Cut Up a Chicken 103

Chicken and Other Poultry Recipes 110

Brine 110
Citrus Marinated Chicken 112
General Tso's Chicken 113
Pan-Seared Chicken and Wild Mushrooms 114
Pan-Seared Duck Breast with Blackberry Veal Stock Reduction 115
Roast Duck Asian Style 116
Szechwan Chicken 118
Tequila Chicken 119

Seafood 120

Seafood Recipes 122

Bill's Shrimp and Feta over Spaghetti Squash 123
Crawfish Egg Rolls 124
Crawfish Etouffee 125
Grilled Fish Tacos 126
Herb Crusted Rock Fish with Sauce Beurre Blanc 127
Pan-Seared Salmon Steaks with Sauce Beurre Blanc 128
Pan-Seared White Fish 129
Poached Salmon with Citrus Butter Sauce 130
Seven Spice Shrimp and Mango Salsa 131
Shrimp Creole 132

Vegetables 134

Methods for Cooking Vegetables 135

Vegetable Recipes 137

    Bruschetta 138
    Chipotles in Adobo Sauce 139
    Green Beans and Butternut Squash 140
    Green Beans with Pecans and Bread Crumbs 141
    Grilled Asparagus with Butter and Lemon 142
    Grilled Eggplant Roll-ups 143
    Mushroom Stuffed Crepes 144
    Spicy Slaw Salad 145

Tubers 146

    Potatoes 146
    Boniato and Sweet Potatoes 147
    Jicama 147
    Parsnips 147
    Sunchokes 148
    Taro Root 148
    Water Chestnuts 148
    Yucca 149

Potato and Other Tuber Recipes 150

    Layered Potato Casserole 151
    Mashed Potatoes 152
    French Fried Potatoes 153
    Oven Roasted Parsnip Puree 154
    Oven Roasted Potatoes 155
    Oven Roasted Root Vegetables 156
    Soy Grilled Sweet Potatoes 157

Pizza 158

Pizza Recipes 159

    Neapolitan Pizza Dough 160
    Pizza Sauce 161
    Pizza Margarite 162

Pasta 163

Basic Pasta 164
Sun-Dried Tomato and Balsamic Pasta Salad 165

A Little Something on the Side 166

Fried Rice 167
Grandma's Hush Puppies 168
Rice Pilaf with Dried Cranberries and Toasted Pine Nuts 169

Pastries and Desserts 170

Pastry and Dessert Recipes 171

Basic Crepes 172
Caramel Sauce 173
Chocolate Mango Ravioli 174
Coconut Sorbet 175
Crème Anglais 176
Crepes with Caramelized Sugar and Orange Butter Sauce 177
Dark Chocolate Truffles 178
Empanadas Pastry 179
Grilled Pineapple 180
Leche Flan 181
Pate Sucree 182
Peach Sunrise 184
Raspberry Coulis 185

Techniques 186

Removing Corn From the Cob: 186
Keeping the Corn Together: 186
Cutting Bell Peppers: 186
Removing the Heat from Chilies: 187
Roasting Bell Peppers and Chilies: 187
Making Flavored Olive Oils: 187
Glossary 188
Index 194

Introduction

For me, cooking has always been a way of expressing myself, an outlet for my creativity. In many ways, cooking is a form of art, just like painting or writing or playing music. The palette available in each case is different, but whether it's color, or language, or musical notes, the artist uses that medium to express their passion. Many variables can influence the creative process. For me, music and cooking have always gone hand in hand. I listen to music when I cook. It can inspire me to create a new dish, and when I serve a meal to my family or friends, the ooh's and aah's are my own version of a standing ovation. The smiles on their faces as they enjoy each bite are my reward.

There are many people and places that have influenced my cooking. My mother has always enjoyed cooking and, as a child, I found the whole process fascinating. Mom grew up in England during the Second World War, and she often had trouble getting what she needed from the stores. Choices were usually limited and butter and meat were real treats when she could get them. When she could, Mom would make bacon sandwiches for me for breakfast and they always tasted so good. I used to wonder how she made them taste so good. Her special twist was to fry one of the slices of bread in the bacon drippings before assembling the sandwich. Wow. It was such a simple thing, but it made such a big difference. Bacon sandwiches are still one of my "comfort foods." When life gets a bit rough and I want something to make me feel better or take me back to simpler times, I indulge in my favorite comfort foods. To this day, when I visit my mother, she makes me bacon sandwiches for breakfast, and I wouldn't have it any other way.

Other staples from Mom's childhood included tomato soup, sausage rolls and Sheppard's pie. In fact, tomato soup may have been my first culinary creation. When I was five years old, I decided I had to learn how to make it. At that time, Campbell's tomato soup was king. But I didn't want it out of a can; I wanted to learn to make it myself. Mom helped me every step of the way, standing with me and instructing me not to turn the heat up too high and to keep stirring. It was like magic.

It wasn't just my mother's English cuisine that influenced me. When I was about 10 years old, my family took a vacation to visit relatives in England and I met my Uncle Julian for the first time. He was born in Hungary and introduced me to Hungarian goulash. It was like nothing I had ever tasted before. Over the years, I've tried many people's goulash, but his is still the best. I've included his recipe in this book, written just the way he showed me all those years ago.

Another fond childhood memory is the first time my family and I went to an Italian restaurant. That first bite of real spaghetti with tomato sauce was like a taste of heaven. I still remember the depth and the richness of the flavors and the impression the whole experience had on me. It made me feel like dancing on the inside.

Professional chefs have also inspired me. I used to watch Julia Child on TV and her show fueled my interest in cooking, even as a teenager. In the early nineties, I discovered Justin Wilson, a Cajun cook with flair, Pierre Franey and Jacques Pepin, two French chefs and many others on PBS. They've each made an impression on me in their own way.

It has taken many years for this love of cooking to find its way to the forefront of my life. In fact, back in the eighties, I did work at Marco Polo, an Italian restaurant in Vienna, Virginia. At that time, I perfected my own spaghetti sauce and I've included that recipe in the book as well.

Early in 2001, I discovered a local cooking school and took a cooking class. I had a great time and was glued to every word the instructor, Bonnie Moore, said. I was pleased when she looked at the pasta we were making and asked me to make 2 more batches. It made me feel special. While I was attending the class, I found out they had a program for volunteer assistants and I couldn't wait to get started. For the next year and a half I assisted every chef I could, as they each had something unique to offer. Then I took a 12-week Basic Culinary Skills course with Kristen Dunn, and several months after that I took a 20-week Semi-Professional Culinary Skills course with Susan Waterston. In that class, we weren't given recipes as much as ingredient lists. There were no standard amounts or measurements given, just ingredients to be used. This approach was designed to help the students develop their skills as well as their taste and not to rely heavily on someone else's idea of the perfect combination of ingredients. These two classes changed my life and opened up a whole new world for me.

This book actually began back in 1995 when I met my best friend, Bill Hittle, at a friend's bachelor party. We both enjoyed music, playing the guitar and cooking. Bill introduced me to a cook from New Orleans by the name of Paul Prudhomme and showed me a book he had called, "Seasoned America". I was hooked. The recipes were fabulous. Bill and I started getting together on weekends and experimenting with recipes. We found that most of our culinary information had come from our mothers, cooking shows, and cookbooks. We wanted to know more. How did people come up with these ideas?

We decided to try creating our own recipes. Sometimes we started from scratch and other times we would take an existing recipe and change it to make it better suit our tastes. We were new to this process and not every creation was a success. Even now I make things that will never end up on the dinner table, let alone in a cookbook, but I love putting my own spin on the foods I cook and I look at the failures as learning opportunities.

The recipes in this book are guidelines. Look at them as a place to start and make them your own. To get the most out of it, concentrate on the techniques as you read through the book, rather then just on the recipes. The recipes in the book are a collection of some of my all time favorites and many new recipes that I have written since I went to school. I hope you enjoy them as much as I have enjoyed developing them.

Remember, cooking is an opportunity to share your creativity with family and friends, and nothing brings people together like food.

Special thanks to my instructors at L'Academie de Cuisine:
    Kristen Dunn
    Susan Watterson

Special thanks to the chefs I have assisted and worked with:
    Stephen Sands
    Bonnie Moore
    Susanna Trilling
    Giuliano Bugialli
    Christine Illich
    Jonathan Krinn at 2941 Restaurant
    Dave Arnold
    Somchet Chumpapo

A very special thank you to:
    My Mom, Shirley;
    My Sister, Liz;
    My Nephew, Mathew;
    My Brother, David and his wife, Mara;
    My Brother-in-Law, Kevin;
    My good friend, Bill Hittle, who did the photograph editing, we have made some great meals together;
    My special friend from England, Marie Ashford;
    My friend and helper, Wendell Givens;
    Shaunia Wallace my best student. And all my other friends who let me cook for them and tasted my culinary creations, and did recipe testing.

A very big and special thanks to Beccy Bauer, my English guru, editor, Sous Chef, and a great friend! Without her help, this book would still be a work in progress! We have also made so many wonder meals, and made to many people happy with our food. That is what cooking is all about.

The Art of Cooking by Technique

The first and most important thing to learn when you start savory cooking is that recipes are simply collections of techniques. Some recipes are considered classic and are supposed to be cooked a particular way with exact measurements. But over time, as a recipe is handed down, the type and amount of ingredients will change to suit the cook's taste.

One important technique to learn is tasting. As food is prepared, it must be tasted throughout the process from the beginning until just before it's served. As a sauce reduces or a stew is braised in the oven, flavors intensify and evolve based on the different spices or herbs used, so tasting throughout the cooking process is key.

When you put a bite of food in your mouth, it starts to dissolve. The action of the saliva in your mouth is just the first step in activating your sense of taste. Your teeth also help you to taste foods by breaking up the big pieces so that they can dissolve more quickly. Next, the taste is picked up by your taste buds. You have about 10,000 of these. The taste buds send the message to the brain, by way of nerves and electrical signals. The brain interprets these signals as tastes.

The taste buds on your tongue are clustered all around the sides, but not in the middle, and pick up four or five main tastes. The four traditional tastes are sweet, sour, salty, and bitter. Scientists are also studying a fifth taste, which they have named umami. The tastes are concentrated on particular areas of the tongue. Sweet tastes, such as sugar or honey, are tasted mainly on the front of the tongue. Sour tastes, like lemons, are tasted on the sides. Salty tastes, such as potato chips or fries, are tasted all around the edges of the tongue. Bitter is tasted on the back of the tongue. Bitter is like the taste of unsweetened chocolate. Most people don't like bitter tastes much. Umami is the most recently discovered taste. It is sometimes described as a meaty or savory taste. It is the taste that is provided by monosodium glutamate (MSG) that is sometimes added to Chinese food.

Taste is a very personal thing. There are varied opinions about which foods taste good and many of these opinions come from the culture in which a person was raised. People in some cultures eat only a vegetarian menu and could not bring themselves to eat a lobster or beef. Other people enjoy eating beef and seafood daily, but wouldn't think of eating a fried grasshopper, which people in some cultures consider a treat.

Another factor that contributes to differences in taste is age. The taste buds on your tongue die out and are replaced about once every two weeks. But, as we grow older, some taste buds are not replaced and the overall number diminishes, so older people have a weaker sense of taste than younger people. This may be why some kids are such fussy eaters - they just have a sharper sense of taste.

Tongue Taste Bud Areas
The areas most sensitive to taste are Bitter, Sour, Salty and Sweet

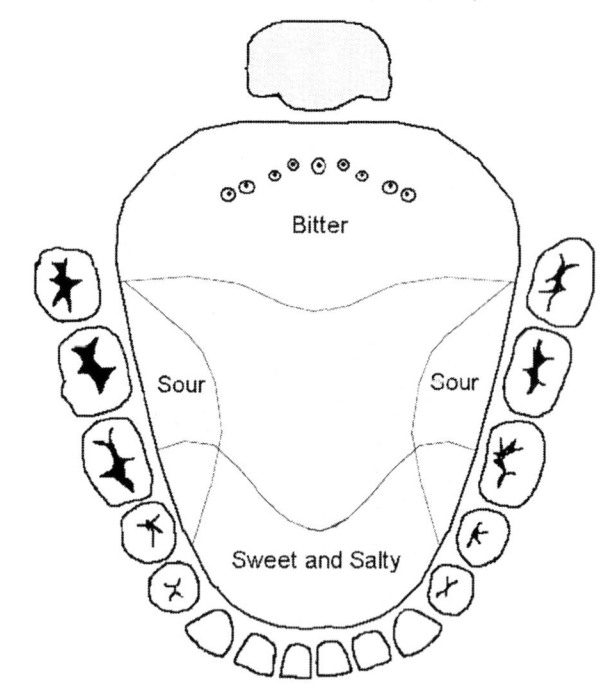

- Bitter
- Sour
- Sour
- Sweet and Salty

In its simplest form, a recipe is a series of techniques for seasoning, blending, and often heating ingredients to end up with a really great tasting meal. Seasoning is adding salt, pepper, spices and/or herbs. By adding a seasoning blend or individual spices and herbs at different times during the cooking process, you affect the flavor of the final dish.

Probably the single largest difference between the fantastic meals you've had at your favorite restaurant and the food you've cooked at home is the amount of seasoning used. Many times it is as simple as adding more salt. It is imperative to have a high quality sea salt and/or kosher salt on hand. Salt brings out an incredible amount of flavor in food. You may find yourself asking, "Is there really a difference in salts?" There are several differences. Kosher salt dissolves more quickly than other salts. High quality sea salt is dried and raked from the ocean and adds a different taste. These types of salt are not as salty as the traditional table salt, owing in part to the preservatives and stabilizers added to iodized salt. One of the best ways to learn how much salt affects the taste of food is to prepare a simple broth or mashed potatoes without adding any salt. Place four to six small dishes on the counter and place a small amount of your broth or potato in each dish. Next, add increasingly larger amounts of salt to each dish, starting with a little in the first and ending with what you think is too much in the last. Then taste them and make notes as you go. This will help you develop and learn about your tastes. It is amazing the difference a quarter teaspoon can make to a dish. Many times when a dish has been prepared and you taste it, you think to yourself, "It tastes good, but it needs something." Chances are that by adding a little more salt, the taste will be more complete. Salt also brings flavors together and makes sweet foods a little sweeter. Many sweet desserts actually call for a pinch of salt.

Some techniques, like stewing, call for adding several spices and/or herbs just once during cooking. To create variations, try combining all of the spices, salt, pepper, and/or dried herbs together. For example, if the recipe calls for sweating or sautéing onions, adding meat and then adding the liquid, spices and or herbs, change the recipe a bit. Create a spice blend by combining the salt, pepper, and all the spices and herbs to create a blend. After sweating the onions, add a portion of the spice blend and let cook for a minute or two to release the oils the spices contain. If the recipe calls for searing the meat, rub the spice blend on the meat and let it marinate a while, if possible, before searing it. By adding the spice blend at different times, the food will taste as if the flavors have been layered. In a stew, the sauce will have a different taste than the meat that was seared in the blend, even though the spices used are the same. The high heat of the searing process will bronze the flavors of the spices causing them to intensify. This is a technique used a lot in Cajun recipes, but also works well with many different styles of cooking. By creating a spice or herb mixture, the flavors start to incorporate before they are used. When the mixture is heated, the essential oils are all released at once and a combined flavor is born.

A nice way to bring out a particular flavor in a dish is to use a combination of dried and fresh herbs. Dried herbs are used when a dish will be cooked for a long time, like a stew. Because the herbs have been dried, their flavors have been concentrated, thus the herbs have to be hydrated in the liquid they are cooked in. Fresh herbs are best used in quick cooking recipes or added in the last few minutes before serving. Fresh herbs are delicate and cannot stand up to a long cooking process without losing their flavor. They can be added in the beginning to flavor oil or butter when heating it in the sauté pan, when the dish is half finished, and again right at the end.

If you have a recipe that you make regularly where all of the dried herbs are added together at the beginning of the cooking process, try adding some more about 2 minutes before serving. If you want a particular herb flavor to be more prominent then the others used, add that herb at the end.

Whenever I have the opportunity to meet someone from a different culture, I ask them what typical seasonings they use in their cooking, since spice blends are part of each ethnic culinary style. Most spice blends include salt and pepper. I have listed several typical groupings of seasonings used in different cuisines from many different parts of the world. As you can see, many of the same seasonings are used in places as diverse as North America, Mexico, and Africa. I have also listed some of my favorite seasoning blends that I use in my cooking.

Typical Italian Seasonings: Thyme, Rosemary, Basil, Crushed Red Pepper, Oregano, and Marjoram.

Typical Cajun Seasonings: Cayenne Pepper, White Pepper, Garlic Powder, Onion Powder, Thyme, Rosemary, Basil, and Marjoram. Many Cajun chefs are now using ground chili powders. See typical southwestern spices below.

Typical Southwestern and Mexican Spices: Various Chilies including Ground Chipotle, New Mexican, Ancho, and Guajilo; Cayenne Pepper; White Pepper; Garlic Powder; Onion Powder; Thyme; Rosemary; Basil; Sage; Cumin; Mexican Oregano and Marjoram.

Typical Asian Spices: Garlic, Ginger, Onion, Cilantro, Lemon Grass, Five Spice Powder, Chilies and many different sauces, such as soy, fish sauce, and Hoisin just to name a few.

Green Chili Soup - Page 53

Pan-Seared and Oven-Roasted Steak w/ French Fries - Page 74

Hungarian Goulash - Page 81

Rack of Lamb Stuffed with Brandy Macerated Apricots - Page 92

6 · The Art of Cooking by Technique

Smoked Brisket – Page 95

Pan-Seared Duck Breast with Blackberry Veal Stock Reduction - Page 115

Pan-Seared White Fish - Page 129

Pizza Margarite - Page 162

8 · The Art of Cooking by Technique

Penne Pasta with Simple Tomato Sauce - Page 41

Fried Rice - Page 167

Peach Sunrise - Page 184

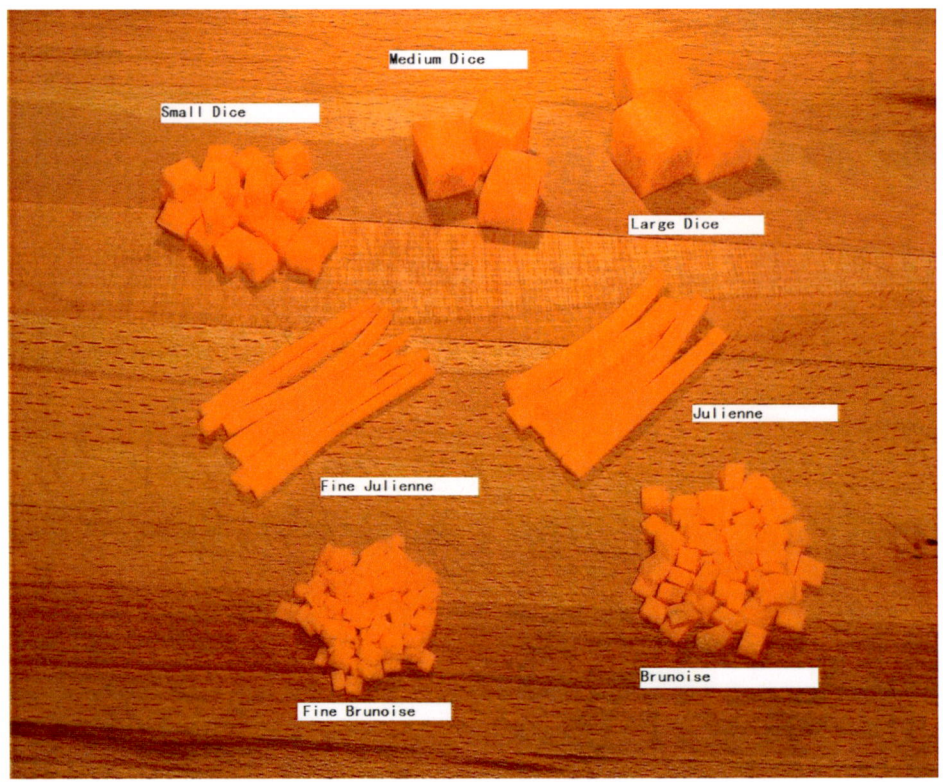

Typical Vegetable Cuts

10 • The Art of Cooking by Technique

The Street Chef's Seasoning Mixtures

Seasoning mixtures are fun to play with. Here are a few of the spice mixtures that I use a lot. They are nice to have on hand when you want to cook something that tastes good, but you don't want to go to a lot of trouble. I use these mixtures on meats and in soups and sauces. It is also nice to add some fresh herbs to the soup or sauce that you are cooking in conjunction with these mixtures about 5 minutes before serving. If you really like a specific spice or herb, try using it to make some of your own creations.

To extend their freshness, store all your spices and seasoning mixes in dark, air-tight containers, in a cool, dark place. Seasoning mixes will keep indefinitely, but will lose their potency after 6 months to a year.

Beef Brisket Rub

(Makes about ¼ Cup)

Ingredients:
1 Tsp	Whole Cumin Seeds
1 Tbsp	Smoked Sweet Paprika
½ Tsp	Chipotle Powder
1 Tsp	Ancho Chili Powder
1 Tbsp	Brown Sugar
1 Tsp	Ground Coriander
¾ Tsp	Onion Powder
½ Tsp	Garlic Powder
1 Tsp	Kosher Salt
1 Tsp	Mexican Oregano
½ Tsp	Freshly Ground Pepper

Heat a small sauté pan over medium heat, leave the pan dry and toast the whole cumin seeds for about 2 to 3 minutes or until fragrant. Pour the cumin seeds into a spice grinder and grind into powder. Combine all ingredients and mix thoroughly.

Creole Seafood Seasoning

(Makes 2 Cups)

Ingredients:
2 Tbsp	Thyme
1/3 Cup + 1 Tbsp	Salt
¼ Cup	Garlic Powder
¼ Cup	Black Pepper
1/3 Cup	Cayenne Pepper
2 Tbsp	Marjoram
1/3 Cup	Sweet Paprika
3 Tbsp	Onion Powder

Combine all ingredients and mix thoroughly. Use on fish, shrimp, crawfish or chicken, or add to soups, stews and sauces for a Creole zing!

Indian Seasoning

(Makes about ¼ Cup)

Ingredients:

- 1 Tsp .... Sea or Kosher Salt
- 4 Tsp .... Smoked Sweet Paprika
- 1 Tbsp .... Ground Black Pepper
- 1 Tsp .... Curry Powder
- 1 Tsp .... Ground Ginger
- 1 Tsp .... Ground Cardamom
- ½ Tbsp .... Cayenne Pepper

Combine all ingredients and mix thoroughly. Use on beef or pork or add to soups, stews and sauces to add a nice Indian character to your food.

Jamaican Seasoning

(Makes about ¼ Cup)

Ingredients:

- 1 Tsp .... Sea or Kosher Salt
- 1 Tsp .... Smoked Sweet Paprika
- ½ Tsp .... Ground Black Pepper
- 2 Tsp .... Sugar
- 1½ Tsp .... All Spice
- ½ Tbsp .... Ground Dried Scotch Bonnet or Habañero Chilies
- ½ Tsp .... Ground Cumin
- ½ Tsp .... Ground Anise
- ½ Tsp .... Ground Ginger
- ¼ Tsp .... Nutmeg
- ¼ Tsp .... Cinnamon
- 1/8 Tsp .... Ground Cloves
- ¼ Tsp .... Ground Cardamom

Combine all ingredients and mix thoroughly. Use on beef, pork or chicken or add to soups, stews and sauces for a Jamaican flair.

Poultry Seasoning
(Makes about ¼ Cup)

Ingredients:
- 6 Tsp .... Salt
- 2 Tsp .... Sweet Paprika
- 1 Tsp .... Cayenne
- 1 Tsp .... Onion Powder
- 1 Tsp .... Garlic Powder
- 1 Tsp .... Ground Black Pepper
- 1 Tsp .... Dried Thyme
- 1 Tsp .... Dried Oregano
- 1 Tsp .... Rubbed Sage
- ½ Tsp .... Ground Cumin

Combine all ingredients and mix thoroughly. Use on chicken, duck or any fowl or add to soups, stews and sauces.

Raz Al Hanout (Moroccan Spice)
(Makes about ¼ Cup)

Ingredients:
- 2 Tsp. .... Ground Ginger
- 2 Tsp .... Ground Cumin
- 1 Tsp. .... Lemon
- 1 Tsp .... Orange Zest
- 1 Tsp .... Lime Zest
- Pinch .... Cayenne Pepper
- 2 Tsp .... Ground Coriander
- ½ Tsp .... Cinnamon
- ½ Tsp .... Allspice
- 1 Tsp .... Salt
- ½ Tsp .... Sugar

Combine all ingredients and mix thoroughly. Use on beef, pork, chicken, duck or any fowl, or add to soups, stews and sauces to add a nice Moroccan flair to your food.

Southwestern Seasoning
(Makes about ½ Cup)

Ingredients:
- 1 Tsp .... Sea or Kosher Salt
- 4 Tsp .... Smoked Sweet Paprika
- 1 Tbsp .... Ground Black Pepper
- 2 Tbsp .... Ground Ancho, Chipotle, or other powder from your favorite chili (not the generic "Chili Powder")
- 2 Tsp .... Ground Cumin
- 2-Tsp .... Mexican Oregano
- 1 Tsp .... Garlic Powder
- 1 Tsp .... Onion Powder
- 1/8 Tsp .... Cinnamon

Combine all ingredients and mix thoroughly. Use on beef or pork or add to soups, stews and sauces for that Southwestern zing.

Steak Seasoning
(Makes about ½ Cup)

Ingredients:
- 2 Tbsp .... Sea or Kosher Salt
- 2 Tbsp .... Smoked Paprika
- 1 Tbsp .... Ground Black Pepper
- 2 Tsp .... Garlic Powder
- 2 Tsp .... Onion Powder
- 1 Tbsp .... Thyme

Combine all ingredients and mix thoroughly. Use on beef or pork or add to soups, stews and sauces.

One of the keys to good cooking I learned in school was the importance of flavors and color. Both are equally important. A dish can have incredible flavor, but if the color of the dish is not pleasing to the eye, then it loses its appeal. Likewise, a dish can have incredible colors but, if it lacks flavor, it will also lose its appeal. Food is a combination of seasoning, texture, flavor, smell, color, taste, texture, and visual impact. The better the balance between these elements, the closer you get to perfection.

The Art of Making Stocks

Without a doubt, one of the most important things you can do to improve your cooking is to start making your own stocks and glazes. I know, I know… I can hear you saying to yourself, "Its just too much trouble," "It takes too long," "I don't have the time." I was very much the same way. I used to use canned broth or bouillon and, for the most part, the recipes would turn out 'okay'. At least that's what I thought until I made them with homemade chicken stock. I just cannot express enough the difference in taste and texture that it will make in your cooking. And I enjoy making stocks. They are easy to make and do not require much attention. If you make large quantities, you can freeze usable amounts in separate containers or plastic bags to be used at your convenience. My freezer at home is mainly used for stocks and I always have at least chicken and veal stock on hand. But for those non-believers, let me share a story:

I frequently cook with friends and I give out recipes when asked. A friend tried making several of my soup recipes but always had the same complaint, "It doesn't taste like yours. It's awful!" In truth, her soups weren't awful, but they definitely weren't what she was expecting. She had tasted my soups and was expecting the same results. I convinced her to try making her own stock. There was the usual initial complaint of it being too hard, etc., but she agreed to give it a try. She admitted afterwards that making the stock was really not that difficult. But the big win came when she used it to make her soup. She loved it! From that moment on, she was sold on stock! No more canned/boxed/freeze dried substitutes for the real thing. She finally understood the difference good stock can make in a recipe.

Simply speaking, stocks, whether beef, chicken, seafood, vegetable, or veal, are flavored water. In fact, when a recipe calls for water, I often replace it with stock because it really impacts the flavor, texture and color of the finished dish. Glazes are reduced stocks and are most often used for making sauces. Reducing the stock to a glaze intensifies the flavor, the color, and the texture. Meat based stocks contain natural gelatins that are released from the bones during cooking. As a meat based stock reduces, the natural gelatins are concentrated and, at room temperature and in the refrigerator, the glaze will jiggle, just like Jell-O!

The stocks you would typically find in use in a professional kitchen are:

- Veal Stock: Sometimes referred to as brown stock, or demi-glaze.
- Beef Stock: Not used as much anymore, but I think it still has some great uses.
- Chicken Stock.
- Shrimp or Fish Stock.
- Vegetable Stock.

In my opinion, homemade stocks and glazes should be used in all soups and sauces. When it comes to making stocks, there aren't hard and fast rules about quantities, but rather a 'set' of ingredients and techniques. When it comes to brown stocks, demi-glazes and glazes, it all starts with bones, marrow, vegetables, herbs and spices. The vegetables, also known as 'mirepoix', consist of onions, carrots, and celery. The herbs and spices, also known as a 'bouquet garni', consist of bay leaves, whole black pepper corns, fresh parsley and thyme. Classically, these are tied up in cheesecloth, but since, with stock, the final product is strained, there is no need to waste the cheesecloth. They can be added individually directly to the pot.

No matter what type of stock you make, the process is basically the same. Let's take a look at that process by starting with the simplest stock – Vegetable Stock.

Vegetable Stock / Stock Basics

I generally make vegetable stock for soups or stews. This type of stock is great to use if you have guests over that are vegetarians. Vegetable stock does not require a long cooking time, so you can make it the same day or a day or so before you need it.

Start with your largest pot, because after you see what a difference it makes in your finished dishes, you will wish you had made more. And what you don't use immediately can be frozen for later use. I generally use a 16-quart stockpot.

For any of the meat based stocks, you fill the pot 2/3 full of either, roasted veal bones, roasted beef bones, chicken parts, shrimp shells and heads if you are lucky enough to get them, or fish parts. For vegetable stock, you obviously skip that step. The remainder of the pot (or the whole pot for vegetable stock) is then filled with 3 parts onion, 2 parts carrots, and 1 part celery. For a 16-quart pot, I generally use about 5 or 6 yellow onions that have been peeled and cut in half, leaving the root end intact. I generally use a small bag of carrots, which I peel and wash under cold water to avoid the transference of any dirt, and about half a bunch of celery, also chopped into large chunks. Then you add about a dozen stems each of fresh parsley and thyme, a couple of bay leaves, and a couple teaspoons of whole peppercorns. You can also add mushrooms for additional flavoring.

Never add salt to your stock because, as it reduces, the concentration of salt will increase and can become overwhelming. For maximum control and flavor enhancement, add salt to the dish you are preparing with the stock, not to the stock itself.

Now fill the stockpot up with cold water. Cold water will draw the most flavors out of the vegetables (and meat) and will produce complex flavors, rich color, and a less cloudy end result. This is because, when a stock starts with cold water and is heated gently to the boiling point, the proteins in the bones and meat will have time to slowly coagulate, clump together, and rise to the surface as foam. This foam can then easily be skimmed off and discarded, leaving the stock clearer.

Turn the heat on to medium to start the cooking and do not cover the pot. Bring the pot just up to a simmer, turn the heat down to low, and cook for the recommend time. While times are approximate, here is my rule of thumb:

Vegetable Stock:.........45 minutes to an hour
Shrimp or Fish Stock: About an hour
Chicken Stock:...........3-4 hours
Beef Stock: ....4-5 hours
Veal Stock: ....8-10 hours

During the cooking process, skim off any fat or foam that appears. After cooking, carefully remove the vegetables (and bones if it is a meat based stock) and strain the stock. Place the strained stock in an ice bath to completely cool. When cooled, remove any fat from the top, place in small containers, and either store in the refrigerator for use in the next week or freeze for future use.

Veal Stock / Beef Stock

Veal stock is the mother of all stocks. It adds incredible flavor to anything it goes into and, from soups to sauces, it will add depth, color and texture. This is by far the most time consuming stock to make, but your efforts will be rewarded. You will need veal bones. Some specialty grocery stores carry them, but your best bet is probably to get them from your butcher. If you are making beef stock, you'll of course use beef bones.

Pre-heat the oven to 450°. Wash the bones under cold water and pat dry. Place the bones on a sheet tray or a large baking dish and bake in the pre-heated oven for 45 minutes to an hour, or until the bones are well browned. For a 16-quart stockpot, I use about 15 to 16 pounds of bones. Remove the bones from the oven, drain and discard any fat.

Place the roasted bones in the stockpot, along with any browned bits left on your tray or baking dish. You can get them to let go of the pan by deglazing with a little water. These browned bits are called 'Fond' in French which means 'bottom'. They have a lot of flavor and should be added to your stock.

Fill the pot 2/3 full with the roasted bones. Then add your vegetables. Since veal and beef stocks cook for such a long time, it is especially important to cut your vegetables into very large chunks. Now add your fresh parsley, thyme, bay leaf and peppercorns.

Next add 1 small can of tomato paste and then fill the stockpot with cold water. Turn the heat on to medium to start the cooking and do not cover the pot. Bring the pot just up to a simmer, turn the heat down to low, and cook for 8 to 10 hours for veal stock or 4 to 5 hours for beef stock. During the cooking process, skim off any fat or foam that appears. After cooking, carefully remove the bones (reserve the bones) and vegetables and strain the stock. Place the strained stock in an ice bath to completely cool. When cooled, remove any fat from the top. At this point you have stock.

To make a demi-glaze (half glaze), place the stock back into the stockpot and place on the stove over medium heat. As soon as the stock starts to simmer, lower the heat and let the liquid reduce by half. Cool the demi-glaze and place it in small containers in the freezer.

With the reserved bones, you can make another batch of stock by following the same procedure as listed above. You will need to replenish the carrots, onions, celery, and the bouquet garni. This second round of stock will not be as rich as the first, but it will be great for adding to stews and soups. When either of these stocks is cooled, they will appear to be like Jell-O, very gelatinous.

Chicken Stock

Depending on the size of your stock pot, you will need anywhere from 5 to 25 pounds of chicken. Chicken backs, necks, thighs, and legs are best. Whenever I buy a whole chicken to cut up for a recipe, I save the remaining carcass in a plastic bag in the freezer. Then when I'm ready to make more stock, I already have a start on the chicken.

Fill the pot about 2/3 full with chicken. Then add 3 parts onions, 2 parts carrots, and 1 part celery, plus your bouquet garni. Add enough COLD water to cover the chicken and vegetables. Heat over moderate heat until it begins to simmer, and then reduce the heat to a low simmer. Simmer for three to four hours, skim the fat and foam from the top, and let cool. Finally, strain the stock through a fine mesh strainer. At this point, the stock can be reduced by half to make a glaze. Refrigerate for up to 3 days or freeze for up to six months.

Shrimp Stock

This is a very easy stock to make if you save any shells you've used when cooking shrimp at home. Simply place any shells in a plastic bag and store them in the freezer. Then they're available whenever you want to make stock. I generally use a 4-quart saucepan, because I do not use shrimp stock that often. Fill your pot 2/3 full with the shrimp shells. Fill the remainder of the pot with 3 parts onion, 2 parts celery, and the bouquet garni. You'll notice there are no carrots in this stock. Carrots impart too much color and too strong a flavor for seafood stock, so they are omitted. Since the stock does not cook long, the vegetables should be cut into a medium dice - about ¼" to ½"dice.

Fill the pot with cold water and place on the stove. Heat the pot to a simmer and let cook for about an hour. Be sure to skim any foam or fat that rises to the top. Strain the stock and place in an ice bath to completely cool. Remove any fat, store in small containers, and freeze until needed. If you eat lobster, you can also save the shells from the lobsters to make lobster stock.

Fish Stock

If you fish or buy whole fish, save all the trimmings (except the innards) and place in a plastic bag in the freezer until you have enough to make stock. Again I do not use a lot of fish stock, so I generally do not make big quantities.

In a 4-quart saucepan, fill the pot 2/3 full with the fish bones, heads, and tails. Fill the remainder of the pot with 3 parts onion, 2 parts celery, and the bouquet garni. As in shrimp stock, the carrots are omitted due to their strong flavor and color. Fill the pot with cold water and place on the stove. Heat the pot to a simmer and let cook for about an hour. Be sure to skim any foam or fat that rises to the top. Strain the stock and place in an ice bath to completely cool. Remove any fat, store in small containers, and freeze until needed.

The Art of Making Sauces

One of the main uses of stock is in the preparation of sauces, and I for one believe just about everything can be made better if you add a little sauce to it. Not all sauces, however, require stock. While there are hundreds, if not thousands of potential sauces, they can all be classified into one of 5 categories that stem from what are called 'Mother Sauces'.

The French are credited with refining the art of sauce-making and they started this classification system with all sauces coming from one of five foundations or 'Mother Sauces'. Those basic sauces are the white sauce, Béchamel; the light stock-based white sauce, Velouté; the brown stock-based Espagnole; the two basic emulsified sauces, Hollandaise and Mayonnaise; and the oil and vinegar-based Vinaigrette.

A few tips to remember when preparing sauces: do yourself a favor and prepare all of the ingredients and have everything ready to add to the pan before you begin. The French have a term for this - Mis en Place – which means putting everything in place before you start. This will make your cooking experience go more smoothly. When adding cream to sauces, always use heavy cream. Heavy cream can withstand high temperatures and is more difficult to break. When using butter, always use unsalted. Salted butter is not as consistent since the amount of salt varies between manufacturers. It is best to add salt directly to the dish you are preparing so you can control the amount. When using tomatoes from a can, make sure they are high quality. And there is nothing wrong with using canned tomatoes; in fact, their quality is more consistent than fresh tomatoes.

Mother Sauces

Béchamel

One ounce of fat and 1 ounce of flour will thicken 1 pint of liquid, so adjust your amounts accordingly.

Ingredients:
1 oz .... Butter
1 oz .... Flour
1 Pint .... Milk

Method:
- Heat a pan over medium heat and melt the butter.
- Slowly add flour, stirring constantly. Add salt and white pepper.
- At this point, for classic Béchamel, you would add an onion studded with cloves but that step is now considered optional.
- Cook ten minutes, then add cold whole milk slowly and stir constantly with a whisk.
- Bring the mixture to a boil and reduce the heat. Taste and adjust the seasoning.

A mixture of flour and fat, as used in the Béchamel sauce, is called a 'roux'. Roux's can be cooked to several stages – White (as in a Béchamel), Blonde (or peanut butter colored), and Brown (or dark chocolate colored). When thickening sauces with a roux, always add cold liquid to the hot roux. This will help in reducing lumps in the sauce. Always cook the flour for at least 10 minutes to cook the flour taste out of the sauce. And remember, the sauce will never reach its ultimate thickness until it reaches a boil.

Velouté

Ingredients:
3 Tbsp .... Butter
3 Tbsp .... Flour
¼ Cup .... Cream
1 .... Egg Yolk Whipped Together with the Cream (Optional)
To Taste .... Salt and Pepper
Bouquet Garni (optional)

Method:
- Heat a pan over medium heat and melt the butter.
- Slowly add flour, stirring constantly. Add salt and white pepper and cook ten minutes.
- Add cream slowly and stir constantly with a whisk.
- Add liaison and heat the mixture over low heat until it thickens. Taste and adjust the seasoning.

Espagnole (Basic Brown Sauce)

Ingredients:

¼ Cup	Butter
1 Clove	Garlic, minced
1 Medium	Onion, chopped
1	Carrot, chopped
¼ Cup	Flour
3 Cups	Beef or Veal Stock
½ Cup	Tomato Puree
1½ Tsp	Fresh Thyme (or ½ Tsp Dried Thyme)
½	Bay Leaf
1 Tsp	Fresh Parsley, chopped
To Taste	Salt and Freshly Ground Pepper

Method:

- Heat a pan over medium heat and sauté the garlic, onion and carrot in the butter until golden, about 5 minutes. Stir in the flour and lower the heat. Cook until the roux is a rich golden brown color, stirring constantly. This should take about 8 to 10 minutes.
- Bring your stock to a boil. Remove the pan with the roux from the heat and add the boiling stock while stirring. Beat with a whisk until the roux is blended into the liquid.
- Blend in the tomato puree and the herbs and simmer partially covered on low heat until the sauce is reduced to 2 cups, approximately 45 to 60 minutes.
- Strain the sauce and season with salt and pepper.

Hollandaise

Hollandaise is a hot emulsified sauce. Out of all of the sauces to make, hollandaise is the easiest to break. Causing a sauce to break means that the eggs and butter separate.

Ingredients:
6 oz	Clarified Butter
1 Tbsp	Hot Water
3	Egg Yolks
Juice of	1 Lemon
To Taste	Salt
Pinch	Cayenne Pepper

Method:
- The butter used in a Hollandaise must be clarified. To clarify butter, place the butter in a pan, melt it, and bring it to a boil. Keep your eyes on the butter. Just before it reaches a boil, it will start to foam on top. That foam is the milk solids. As the butter reaches a boil, there will be lots of small bubbles created by the water in the butter evaporating. The bubbles get larger as more and more of the water evaporates. The milk solids will brown and sink to the bottom. At this point, remove the pan and drain the clarified butter into a separate container. Discard the left over milk solids. Clarified butter has a higher smoking point and can be used for cooking foods where high heat is essential.
- Set up a double boiler. If you don't have a double boiler, you can make one. Simply fill a 3 to 5-quart saucepot with about 1½" of water and heat it to a simmer.
- In a heat-proof bowl that is bigger around than the top of your pot, beat the egg yolks together and then place the bowl over the simmering water. Be careful not to let the mixture get too hot. The easiest way to do this is to place the bowl over the water for several minutes and then remove it to let it cool slightly.
- Constantly whisk the egg yolks until they are pale yellow and start to thicken. Then, slowly drizzle the clarified butter into the egg mixture. Remember to remove the bowl from the heat now and then, since if the sauce gets too hot, it will break.
- As the sauce thickens, add the lemon juice, salt and cayenne.

Vinaigrette

Vinaigrettes are simply cold emulsified sauces and are generally comprised of acid, fat, an emulsifier, and aromatics. Many options are available within these four categories. Let's start wit the acid. Usually this means vinegar, citrus juice, or wine. If using vinegar, you have many choices including red wine, balsamic, sherry, and rice wine vinegars just to name a few. There are so many different types of vinegar available now that they are just too many to list. Vinaigrettes can also be made with lemon, lime, orange or other citrus juices without vinegar or in conjunction with vinegar. Wines, including red, white and fortified wines such as Port and Sherry, can also be used instead of vinegar.

For your choice of fats, the list is long and varied as well and includes such options as olive oil, sesame oil, vegetable oil or one of the many nut oils that are available. As in any emulsified sauce, be careful when adding the oil. Adding the oil too fast will break the sauce. Just slowly drizzle in the oil as you whisk or blend the vinaigrette.

The third ingredient in a classic vinaigrette is an emulsifier. The most common emulsifiers are mustard, sour cream, and egg yolks.

The last ingredients are the aromatics and/or seasonings, such as herbs, shallots, garlic, and just about any spices that you care to use. Oh, and please don't forget the salt and pepper.

The basic formula for a vinaigrette is 1 part acid (vinegar or fruit juice) to 3 parts fat or oil plus your emulsifier and aromatics. With those final ingredients, keep in mind that you want a nicely balanced vinaigrette.

I have listed the vinaigrettes that I generally use. The best way to totally emulsify the vinaigrette is to use a blender. But I generally just use a whisk because I am lazy and don't want to have to clean the blender.

I really like playing with vinaigrettes; there are so many ways to change them. You can add things like sun-dried tomatoes, chilies, mushrooms, caramelized onions and garlic. When I am making a multi-course meal, I try to think about what I am serving and try to match the vinaigrette to the meal. One way of doing this is to use a common ingredient from the meal.

Salads can be very creative. Try adding sliced apples, or pears sliced thinly the length of the fruit and fanned out. When plating the salad, always use an odd number of larger items, such as 3 or 5 apple slices, as it keeps the dish interesting. Odd numbers have been shown to be more pleasing to the eye. Try adding roasted nuts such as peanuts, pecans, walnuts, hazelnuts, pine nuts, or cashews. The nuts add an interesting bit of texture and color. I also use dried cranberries during the holiday season. As I sit here, all kinds of things come to mind.

As a final touch, when I serve salads, I generally make fresh croutons. There is no substitution for freshly made croutons and they are so easy to make.

To make fresh croutons:

- Start with a loaf of your favorite bread. Remove a slice or more (depending on the number of people you are serving) and cut the slices into bite-sized pieces.
- Place about 2 inches of oil in a sauce pan and heat until the oil reaches 285°.
- Cook the bread in small batches until golden brown, about 1 to 2 minutes. Remove and drain on a wire rack or on paper towels and season with salt and pepper or your favorite seasoning blend.
- Let cool and use to top your favorite salad or bowl of soup. These are sinfully delicious!

Vinaigrette Recipes

Champagne Vinaigrette

<u>Ingredients:</u>

1 Tbsp	Dijon Mustard
1 Clove	Garlic, minced
1 Tbsp	Shallots, finely chopped
To Taste	Salt and Pepper
1 Tbsp	Fresh Herbs (your choice)
3 Tbsp	Champagne Vinegar
6 Tbsp	Olive Oil

<u>Method:</u>

- In a mixing bowl, add the Dijon mustard, garlic, shallots, salt, pepper, herbs and Champagne Vinegar. Mix well to incorporate.
- Start whisking and slowly add the olive oil. Mix until an emulsion is formed. The recipe can be doubled or tripled to make the amount needed for any amount of salad greens that you are dressing.
- Serve over fresh greens.

Rice Wine Vinaigrette

<u>Ingredients:</u>

2 Tsp	Dijon Mustard
1 Tbsp	Garlic, minced
1 Tbsp	Shallots, finely chopped
To Taste	Salt and Pepper
1 Tbsp	Fresh Herbs (your choice)
½ Tsp	Sugar
¼ Tsp	Red Pepper Flakes
1/3 Cup	Rice Wine Vinegar
2/3 Cup	Extra Virgin Olive Oil

<u>Method:</u>

- In a mixing bowl, add the Dijon mustard, garlic, shallots, salt, pepper, herbs, sugar, pepper flakes, and rice wine vinegar. Mix well to incorporate.
- Start whisking and slowly add the olive oil. Mix until an emulsion is formed. The recipe can be doubled or tripled to make the amount needed for any amount of salad greens that you are dressing.
- Serve over fresh greens.

Sauce Recipes

Alfredo Sauce

Ingredients:

4 Tbsp.	Butter
2 to 3 Cloves	Garlic, minced (optional)
1 to 1½ Cups	Cream
½ Cup	Parmesan Cheese or Pecorino Cheese, grated
¼ Tsp	Fresh Ground Nutmeg
To Taste	Salt and Pepper
	Fresh Basil or your favorite herb for garnish

Method:

- In a heavy-bottomed sauté pan, heat butter over medium heat. Add garlic, if desired and sauté for 1 minute.
- Add cream and bring to a simmer.
- Add cheese and mix constantly until slightly thickened.
- Add nutmeg and taste for seasoning. Add more salt, pepper or nutmeg if desired.
- To check for consistency, us a piece of al dente pasta and see how it coats the pasta. If the sauce is too thick, add a little pasta water or more cream.
- Taste and adjust seasonings.
- Serve over the pasta of your choice with a chiffonade of basil on top.

Variations on a Theme:

- Add chipotle in adobe sauce and/or chorizo sausage for a southwestern flavor.
- Add grilled chicken breast, fresh herbs and sun-dried tomatoes for a more Italian flare.

Barbecue Sauce

Ingredients:

1 Cup	Ketchup
1 Tbsp	Molasses
½ Tsp	Hot Sauce
½ Tsp	Worcestershire Sauce
1 Med. to Large	Shallot, roasted
3 Cloves	Garlic, roasted
1 Tbsp	Golden Cane Syrup
1 Tbsp	Brown Sugar
½ Tsp	Ground Ginger
¼ Tsp	Cardamom
1 Tbsp	Jamaican or Southwestern Seasoning
1 Tsp	Cumin
1 Tbsp	Ground Ancho Chili Powder
To Taste	Pepper

Method:

- Mix all ingredients together and let macerate for at least 1 hour.

Tip: Will keep for several weeks in the refrigerator.

Barbecue Sauce Basics - Mustard Based

Ingredients:

1-2 Tbsp.	Olive Oil
1 Med. to Large	Shallot, finely chopped
1 to 2 Cloves	Garlic, finely chopped
¼ to ½ Cup	Apple Cider Vinegar
1 Cup	Mustard (I like coarse mustard)
½ Tsp	Hot Sauce
1 Tbsp	Brown Sugar
1 Tsp	Paprika
½ Tbsp	Ground Cayenne Pepper
To Taste	Salt and Pepper

Method:

- Heat a 2-quart saucepan over medium heat. Add the olive oil and shallots and let sweat until softened.
- Add the garlic and cook 2 to 3 minutes or until fragrant.
- Deglaze with the apple cider vinegar. Let reduce for 3 minutes.
- Add the remaining ingredients and let cook for about 20 minutes.
- Strain though cheesecloth or a metal strainer. The sauce will keep for several weeks in the refrigerator.

Barbecue Sauce Basics - Tomato Based

<u>Ingredients:</u>

1-2 Tbsp.	Olive Oil
1 Med. to Large	Shallot, finely chopped
1 to 2 Cloves	Garlic, finely chopped
¼ to ½ Cup	Apple Cider Vinegar
1 Cup	Ketchup
1 to 2 Tbsp	Molasses
½ Tsp	Hot Sauce
1 Tbsp.	Brown Sugar
1 Tsp.	Cumin, toasted
1 Tsp.	Paprika
1 Tbsp.	Ground Ancho Chili Powder or 1 to 2 whole ancho chiles re-hydrated
To Taste	Salt and Pepper

<u>Method:</u>

- Heat a 2-quart saucepan over medium heat. Add the olive oil and shallots and let sweat until softened.
- Add the garlic and cook 2 to 3 minutes or until fragrant.
- Deglaze with the apple cider vinegar. Let reduce for 3 minutes.
- Add the remaining ingredients and let cook for about 20 minutes.
- Strain though cheesecloth or a metal strainer. The sauce will keep for several weeks in the refrigerator.

<u>Variations on a Theme:</u>

- Use roasted garlic or roasted shallots. Try white, yellow, purple or Vidalia onions. Try using cane sugar instead of, or in conjunction with, the brown sugar. Try different chilies, such as chipotle, New Mexican or any other chilies that you like. Try different vinegars, such as rice wine, red wine, balsamic or champagne. Add different spices like cayenne, Mexican oregano, or thyme. Try using different mustards or adding ginger. You could even add Coca-Cola!

Barbecue Sauce Basics - Vinegar Based

Ingredients:
1 Cup .... Apple Cider Vinegar
1 to 2 Tbsp .... Sugar
1 Tsp .... Red Pepper Flakes, more if you like it hot
1 Med. to Large ... White or Red Onion, finely chopped
1 to 2 Cloves .... Garlic, finely chopped
To Taste .... Salt and Pepper

Method:
- Place the vinegar in a bowl, add the remaining ingredients and let macerate for at least 1 hour.

Variations on a Theme:
Try white, yellow, purple or Vidalia onions. Other chilies can be used instead of red pepper flakes, such as cayenne, chipotle or your favorite chilies. Also try different vinegars.

Blackberry Pan Sauce

Ingredients:
1 Tbsp .... Shallots, finely chopped
To Taste .... Salt and Pepper
½ Cup .... Red Wine
1 Pint .... Fresh Blackberries
1 Cup .... Veal Stock or Chicken Stock

Method:
- Heat pan over medium-high heat. Add the shallots, salt, pepper, and red wine of your choice. Let reduce until the pan is almost dry.
- Add the blackberries and cook until softened, then smash into a paste. Cook for 2 to 3 minutes.
- Add the veal or chicken stock and cook until thickened. Strain through a fine mesh strainer and pour over grilled chicken, pork or serve with Pan Seared Duck Breast. (See recipe in 'Chicken and Other Poultry Recipes' section of the book.)

Brandy Veal Stock Reduction

(Accompanies Rack of Lamb Stuffed with Brandy Macerated Apricots Recipe in the 'Lamb Recipes' section of the book.)

Ingredients:

2 Tbsp.	Butter
	Any left over scraps of meat from cleaning the bones
To Taste	Salt and Pepper
1	Shallot, finely chopped
1 Tsp	Thyme
4 to 6	Dried Apricots, finely chopped
1/3 Cup	Reserved Brandy or Cognac from macerating the apricots you used to stuff the lamb. You may need a little more brandy to make up a 1/3 of a cup.
1 Cup	Veal Demi-Glaze

Method:

- Drain any fat out of the sauté pan that you cooked the rack of lamb in. Heat the pan over medium-high heat, add a tablespoon of the butter to the pan and cook the butter until it starts to foam and turns slightly brown in color.
- Season the leftover meat scraps with salt and pepper, add to the pan, and cook until caramelized. Add the shallots and let cook for 2 minutes. Deglaze the pan with the reserved brandy. Add the thyme and the chopped apricots.
- Cook the brandy mixture until the pan is almost dry. Add the veal demi-glaze and reduce by half. Strain the sauce, and add back to the sauté pan off the heat. Swirl in the butter until incorporated and spoon over the rack of lamb.

Chipotle Tomato Salsa

(Makes 3 cups)

Ingredients:

20	Roma Tomatoes
¼ Cup	Extra Virgin Olive Oil
Juice of ½	Lime
¼ Cup	Red Wine Vinegar
4 Cloves	Garlic, minced
½ Medium	White Onion, finely chopped and rinsed in cold water
½ Cup	Cilantro, finely chopped
4 to 6	Chipotle Chilies in Adobo Sauce, finely chopped (see recipe or purchase canned)
1 Tbsp.	Salt
To Taste	Fresh Pepper
Good Pinch	Sugar

Method:

- Cut tomatoes in half, remove seeds and roast under broiler or on grill, skin side up, until skin is charred. Let cool.
- Remove skin and cut up into ½" dice.
- Place in bowl, add remaining ingredients, and stir to incorporate.

Garlic and Mushroom Butter Cream Sauce

(Serves 8)

Ingredients:
¼ oz. Pkg.………Dried Mushrooms soaked until softened or fresh mushrooms
6 Tbsp. ……………..Butter
2 Tbsp. ……………..Shallots, chopped
3 Medium………….Garlic Cloves, minced
3 oz. ………………..Heavy Whipping Cream

Method:
- Finely mince the mushrooms and cook them in 2 tablespoons of the butter. This should take about 5 minutes. Remove the mushrooms and set aside.
- In the same pan, sweat the shallots and garlic in the remaining 4 tablespoons of butter. Be careful not to let the shallots and garlic brown, or the taste will turn bitter.
- Add the mushrooms to the shallots and garlic and heat together for about 2 minutes. Stir in the cream and reduce for 2-3 minutes. Serve immediately.

I have served this sauce on homemade ravioli stuffed with ricotta, feta, mushrooms, and spinach. It was excellent!

Lemon Veal Glaze Sauce

Ingredients:
½ Cup	White Wine
1	Shallot, finely chopped
Zest of	1 Lemon
Juice of	1 Lemon
½ Cup	Veal Demi-Glaze
To Taste	Salt and Pepper
Optional	Thyme, Fresh Parsley, Herbs de Provence
1 Tbsp	Butter

Method:
- If you have sautéed chicken, veal, pork or fish, place the chopped shallots into the pan you cooked the meat in, then add white wine to deglaze the pan. If you are making the sauce without having sautéed any meat first, heat the pan over medium-high heat, add the shallots and white wine together and bring to a low boil.
- Add the lemon zest and let the wine mixture reduce until the pan is almost dry.
- Add the lemon juice and veal glaze, stir and taste.
- Swirl the pan and add salt and pepper. Let cook 1 minute and taste for seasoning.
- Add fresh thyme or other fresh herbs and let simmer 2 more minutes.
- Remove from heat and swirl in the butter.
- Strain sauce through a fine mesh strainer and serve over the meat of your choice.

Lime Butter Sauce

Ingredients:

1 Tbsp	Shallots, finely chopped
To Taste	Salt and Pepper
Juice of	2 Limes
Zest of	1 Lime
4 to 6 Tbsp.	Cold Butter, cut into small cubes
1 Tbsp.	Fresh Herbs (Optional)

Method:

- Heat the pan over medium-high heat; add the shallots, salt, pepper, juice of two limes and half of the zest. Let reduce until the pan is almost dry.
- Remove the pan from the heat and slowly add the butter, stirring constantly. As soon as the butter is melted, add additional butter a little at a time until all the butter has been incorporated.
- If using herbs, add them just before serving.
- This sauce works well with poached, baked or fried fish. Also works well with grilled chicken or pork.

Mango Salsa

<u>Ingredients:</u>

3	Mangos, diced
¼ Cup	White Onion, finely diced
3-4 Tbsp	Cilantro, chopped
1 Large	Red or Green Jalapeño, seeded and finely diced (you can use your favorite chili. If you like it really hot, try a Scotch Bonnet or Habanera.)
Juice of 1	Lime
Pinch	Salt and Pepper
Pinch	Sugar

<u>Method:</u>

- Cut all the ingredients as directed and place in a bowl.
- Mix to combine and let macerate for at least one hour, stirring every 20 minutes.

Red Wine Pan Sauce

<u>Ingredients:</u>

1 Tbsp	Shallots, finely chopped
To Taste	Salt and Pepper
½ Cup	Red Wine
1 Tbsp.	Fresh Herbs (optional)
½ Cup	Veal Stock
1 Tbsp.	Cold Butter, cut into small cubes (optional)
2 Tbsp.	Cream (optional)

<u>Method:</u>

- Heat pan over medium-high heat. Add the shallots, salt, pepper, and red wine of your choice. Let reduce until the pan is almost dry. Add herbs of your choice.
- Add the veal stock (chicken stock may be substituted). Let the sauce reduce by at least half or until it reaches your desired consistency.
- Remove from heat and swirl in the butter and cream if using.

Simple Tomato Sauce

Ingredients:

2 Tbsp	Olive oil
3 Tbsp	Red Onions, finely chopped
To Taste	Salt and Pepper
1 Clove	Garlic, minced
2 Tbsp	Carrot, finely chopped
1 Tbsp	Celery, finely chopped
8 Tbsp	Fresh Basil
½ Tsp	Red Pepper Flakes
3 Tbsp	Tomato Paste
½ Cup	Red Wine
½ Cup	Chicken Stock
1 - 28 oz. Can	Good Quality Roma Tomatoes
	Fresh Basil and Olive Oil for garnish

Method:

- In a heavy-bottomed Dutch oven, heat olive oil over medium heat.
- Sweat onions until clear, adding salt and pepper while cooking.
- Add the garlic and cook until slightly golden in color.
- Add the carrots and celery and cook until softened, about 10 minutes.
- Raise the heat to medium-high and add half of the fresh basil and red pepper flakes and all the tomato paste. Cook until dark red.
- Deglaze with the red wine. Cook until reduced by half.
- Add the chicken stock.
- Add the can of tomatoes and crush.
- Add salt and pepper to taste and simmer at least ½ hour.
- Taste and adjust the seasonings.
- Add the remaining fresh basil.
- If you like the sauce smooth, get the boat motor out and puree it. Taste and adjust the seasonings.
- Serve over the pasta of your choice topped with a chiffonade of basil on top and a drizzle of your best olive oil.

Tip: The longer this cooks, the better it gets.

Spirit Pan Sauce

Ingredients:

1 Tbsp	Shallots, finely chopped
To Taste	Salt and Pepper
½ Cup	Whiskey, Cognac, Port, Apple Brandy, Apricot Brandy or whatever spirit you like
1 Tbsp.	Fresh Herbs (optional)
½ Cup	Veal Stock
1 Tbsp.	Cold Butter, cut into small cubes (optional)
2 Tbsp.	Cream (optional)

Method:

- Heat pan over medium-high heat. Add the shallots, salt, pepper, and spirit of your choice. Let reduce until the pan is almost dry. Add herbs of your choice.
- Add the veal stock (chicken stock may be substituted). Let the sauce reduce by at least half or until it reaches your desired consistency.
- Remove from heat and swirl in butter and cream if using.

Variations on a Theme:
Garlic can also be added.

Tomatillo Salsa

(Makes 3 cups)

Ingredients:

15 to 20	Ripe Tomatillos, husks removed and roughly chopped (Tomatillos are ripe when they are a pale yellow-green and have filled out their husk)
1 Tbsp.	Tequila
Juice of ½	Lime
½ Cup	White Onion, finely chopped and rinsed in cold water
¼ Cup	Cilantro, finely chopped
6	Serrano Chilies, seeded and finely chopped
1 Tsp.	Salt

Method:

- In a blender or food processor, add all ingredients and pulse until the mixture becomes a coarse puree.
- Taste and adjust the salt.

Tomato Concasse Sauce

(Concasse is a French term that refers to coarsely chopped tomatoes.)

Ingredients:
- Olive oil
- Onions or Shallots, finely chopped
- Salt and Pepper
- Garlic
- Bouquet Garni
- Tomato sauce or chopped tomato

You'll notice I haven't listed quantities here. This recipe is your chance to make the final product your own. Work with these ingredients and use amounts that result in a sauce that appeals to you.

Method:
- Heat a pan over medium heat, add the olive oil and sweat the onions or shallots until tender. Always add a little salt, as this helps the onions or shallots weep or release their liquid.
- Add the garlic and the Bouquet Garni.
- Add the chopped tomato or tomato sauce and season with salt and pepper.
- Simmer about 20 minutes or until desired consistency. Taste and adjust the seasonings before serving.

Tip: This sauce can be used over chicken, or pork, or you can make a batch and add it to soups or stews. You can serve it over deep-fried fish too. Use any white fish such as haddock, red snapper, or trout. Dredge the fish in flour, drench the floured fish fillets in beaten egg, and roll into some bread crumbs seasoned with oregano or other Italian herbs. Either pan fry or deep fry the fillets in vegetable oil at 350° until golden brown and crisp. Place on platter, and spoon the Tomato Concasse on top. Garnish with fresh chopped parsley.

Tomato Vodka Sauce

Ingredients:

2 Tbsp	Olive Oil
2 Medium	Onions, finely chopped
To Taste	Salt and Pepper
2 Tsp. Each	Dried Thyme, Basil and Oregano
2 Tsp.	Red Pepper Flakes
3 Tbsp	Tomato Paste
½ Cup	Vodka
2 - 28 oz. Cans	Good Quality Roma Tomatoes
1 Large	Bay Leaf
2 to 3 Cloves	Garlic, minced
½ Cup	Parmesan Cheese or Pecorino Cheese, grated
½ Cup	Cream
	Fresh Basil and Olive Oil for garnish

Method:

- In a heavy-bottomed Dutch oven, heat olive oil over medium heat.
- Sweat onions until clear, adding salt and pepper while cooking.
- Raise the heat to medium-high and add HALF of the dried herbs and red pepper flakes, and all the tomato paste. Cook until dark red, about 5-10 minutes.
- Deglaze with half of the vodka. Cook until dry.
- Add both cans of tomatoes and crush.
- Add bay leaf and the remaining dried herbs and red pepper flakes, garlic, cheese, and more salt and pepper.
- Simmer at least 1 hour. Taste and adjust the seasonings.
- Add remaining vodka and cook an additional half hour. If the sauce becomes too thick, add a little chicken stock to thin it.
- If you like the sauce smooth, get the boat motor out and puree it.
- At the very end, add the cream, taste and adjust the seasonings.
- Serve over the pasta of your choice with a chiffonade of basil on top and a drizzle of your best olive oil.

Tip: The longer this cooks, the better it gets.

Wild Mushroom Sauce

Ingredients:

1 Pkg.	Dried Porcini Mushrooms (.35 oz.)
1 Pkg.	Dried Chanterelle Mushrooms (.35 oz.)
1 Pkg.	Dried Morel Mushrooms (.35 oz.)
	Boiling Water
2 Tbsp.	Butter
To Taste	Salt and Pepper
¼ Cup	Brandy
2 Cups	Homemade Beef Stock
2 Tbsp.	Cream

Method:

- Place the mushrooms in a large bowl and pour boiling water over them. Let stand in the boiling water until they are soft (about 15-20 minutes.)
- In a 10" skillet, sauté the mushrooms in 1 Tbsp. of the butter. Season with salt and pepper and cook until browned.
- Deglaze the pan with the brandy and reduce until almost dry. Add the beef stock and cook until slightly thickened. Add the cream and the remaining tablespoon of butter and stir until combined.
- Serve over your favorite cut of meat prepared to your liking.

Tip: To serve with chicken, use your favorite chicken stock in place of the beef stock.

The Art of Making Soups

A wonderful use of homemade stocks is in making soup. Most soups use chicken stock as a base. While you can use water instead, you'll find your soups don't have the same depth of character and flavor that soups made with stock will have.

There are many different types of soups, including cream or milk based soups; purees that are processed until they are a smooth consistency; chowders which are a thick, rich soup containing chunks of food; bisques which are thick, creamy soups usually made from shellfish, but sometimes made of pureed vegetables; and Consommés or clear broths. There are recipes in this section for each of these styles. Try them out. Once you master the basic techniques, you can adjust ingredients and seasonings to make just about any kind of soup you like.

One of the things that vary greatly from one soup to another is the thickness. There are many things you can add to thicken a soup. Cream gives a soup really rich flavors and a smooth mouth feel. Legumes, potatoes, or rice can be added diced (like the potatoes in chowder), whole (like the rice in bisques) or pureed to add thickness. Béchamel or volute sauces, which are roux based sauces, will also thicken any soup.

When making soup, the use of older vegetables is quite common. As vegetables age, they loose water and the flavor intensifies. Roasting can also intensify the taste and texture of vegetables. The roasted vegetables should be added towards the end of the cooking process if you want them to be chunky; since additional cooking time would further break them down and they would disintegrate into the soup. If you are doing a pureed soup, you can add them much earlier. All vegetables should be cut to similar sizes so that they'll cook more uniformly. This is another way of adding variety. Uncooked vegetables can be added at the beginning of the cooking process and roasted vegetables can be added at the end to produce two entirely different flavors and textures.

Clarified Soups

Clarified soups or stocks are used differently in many ethnic styles of cooking.

Chinese chefs clarify chicken stock for egg drop soup, hot and sour soup and Wonton soup. Vietnamese chefs use it in Pho soup. The French use it in consommés.

To make clarified stock, you will need to prepare a raft. A raft is a collection of ingredients that floats on top of the stock base. The following amounts will clarify 8 cups of stock.

Ingredients:
- 8 Cups .... Stock of your choice – Chicken, Veal, Beef, Fish, Shrimp
- .... Mirepoix (1 medium yellow onion, 2 carrots, 1 stalk of celery)
- .... Bouquet Garni
- 2-4 oz. .... Ground Meat (The best choice is meat to match the stock – if using chicken stock, use ground chicken, etc.)
- 1 Tsp. .... Lemon Juice
- 4 .... Egg Whites, loosely whipped together

Method:
- Place room temperature stock in large pan with Mirepoix, bouquet garni, ground meat and lemon juice.
- Turn heat on and add the whipped egg whites. The egg whites should be 2" thick.
- Do not stir. The egg whites will capture all of the sediment and impurities as they cook.
- Simmer 30 to 60 minutes. When done, ladle the clarified broth through the egg raft and pass through a chinois or strainer lined with cheesecloth moistened with water. If dry cheesecloth is used, the cheesecloth will absorb a lot of the flavor, so be sure to moisten it first.

Meats in Soups

When adding meat to soups, I usually sear the meat being added before adding any vegetables or liquid. I do this for two reasons. The first is to develop fond, which refers to the brown bits at the bottom of the pan. The second is to develop the flavor of the meat, increasing the amount of flavor that it adds to the soup.

Garnish for Soups

Adding a garnish to your soup just before it is served can add a little zing or flair and can spice up the presentation. Garnishes come in many shapes and sizes. Some of the more popular toppings are: bacon, crisp potatoes, potato waffles, pasta, fresh herbs, fried herbs, spices or spice blends, croutons, crispy tortilla strips, or even a nice dollop of crème fraiche or sour cream.

Soup Recipes

Champagne Soup with Smoked Chicken

(Serves 8)

Ingredients:

½ Tbsp.	Butter
1 Tbsp.	Olive Oil
½ Medium	Onion, cut into a small dice
3 Cloves	Garlic, roasted
3 Cups	Champagne
Pinch	Cayenne
Dash	White Pepper
2 Tsp.	Raw Sugar
3 Tbsp.	Dried Tarragon
5 Cups	Chicken Stock
Juice of	1 Lemon
2 Tbsp.	Cornstarch, mixed with 1 Tbsp of water
1 Cup	Half and Half, or for a richer soup, use heavy cream
	Seasoned, Smoked Chicken, cut on the bias in thin slices for garnish

Method:

- Pre-heat a large Dutch oven over medium heat. Add the butter and olive oil. Add the onions, and roasted garlic and let sweat until clear and soft. Deglaze with the Champagne, and let reduce by half.
- Add the Cayenne, white pepper, sugar, and tarragon. Let cook until fragrant.
- Add the chicken stock and the lemon, bring to a boil, and add the cornstarch mixture. The soup will have to come to a low boil to cause the cornstarch to thicken the soup. Once the soup has thickened, reduce the heat to low and add the half and half or cream and let it cook until warm.
- Garnish with sliced chicken and serve with some homemade croutons and crisp, crumbled bacon.

Tip: This soup goes nicely with a chicken or turkey club sandwich.

Cream of Mushroom Soup

Ingredients:

¾ to 1 Lb.	Mixed Mushrooms, sliced
2 Tbsp	Olive Oil
3 Tbsp	Butter
2	Shallots, finely chopped
1 Clove	Garlic, minced
1 Tbsp	Dried Tarragon
½ Cup	Sherry
2 Cups	Chicken Stock, or Beef Stock
1 Cup	Heavy Cream
To Taste	Salt and Pepper
	Fresh Tarragon for garnish

Method:

- Clean the mushrooms and slice into bite-sized pieces.
- Heat a sauté pan over high heat and add a splash of olive oil and a little butter. Sear the mushrooms in small batches. If you add all the mushrooms at once, you will boil them in their own juices. Add more butter and olive oil if needed. Remove from the heat and let cool.
- Heat a 4-quart pan over medium heat.
- Add the olive oil and sweat the shallots until clear. Add the garlic and tarragon and cook until fragrant. Raise the heat to high.
- Add the sherry and cook until reduced by 1/3.
- Add the chicken stock, the sliced mushrooms and the cream and cook until warmed through, about 10 to 15 minutes.
- Garnish with fresh tarragon and serve. You can also top with a dollop of crème fraiche or sour cream.

Green Chili Soup

Ingredients:

Splash + 2 Tbsp	Olive Oil
4	Chicken Thighs, seasoned with Adobo Seasoning (available at most super markets)
1 Medium	White Onion, finely chopped
3 Tsp.	Mexican Oregano
1 Tsp	Whole Cumin Seeds, toasted and ground
¾ Cup	White Wine
1 Clove	Garlic, minced
3 Large	Tomatillos chopped into ½" dice
1 Can (4 oz.)	Green Chilies
To Taste	Salt and Pepper
2 ½ Cups	Chicken Stock
2 Tbsp	Fresh Cilantro, for garnish

Method:

- Heat a sauté pan over high heat, and add a splash of olive oil. Sear the chicken on both sides until golden brown. Remove and let cool. When cool enough to touch, slice into bite sized pieces.
- Heat a 4-quart pan over medium heat.
- Add 2 tablespoons of olive oil and sweat the onions until clear. Add the oregano and cumin and cook until fragrant. Raise the heat to high.
- Add the white wine and cook until reduced by half.
- Add garlic and the tomatillos's and cook for 10 minutes.
- Reduce the heat to medium. Add the green chiles and season with salt and pepper.
- Add the chicken stock and the sliced chicken and cook until the chicken is warmed through, about 10 to 15 minutes.
- Garnish with fresh cilantro and serve. You can also top with a dollop of crème fraiche or sour cream and fresh fried tortilla strips.

Variations on a Theme:

Try adding some roasted corn.

Hearty Beer & Cheese Soup

Ingredients:

2 Tbsp.	Butter
¼ Cup	Olive Oil
¼ Lb.	Pancetta, diced
2 Large	Russet Potatoes, diced
½ Cup	Red Pepper, minced
1	Carrot, chopped
½	Onion, chopped
½ Cup	Flour
2 ½ Cups	Chicken Stock
2 Cups	Veal Stock
16 oz.	Cheddar Cheese, grated
12 oz	Full-Bodied Beer
To Taste	Salt and Pepper
¼ Cup	Cream
¼ Tsp	Tabasco or your favorite vinegar or vinegar based hot sauce
1/8 Tsp	Worcestershire Sauce
Garnish	You can use Parmesan cheese, croutons, mini potato pancakes, fried pancetta, minced herbs, etc.

Method:

- Melt the butter in a large pot. Add the olive oil and allow it to heat through. Add the pancetta and cook until crisp.
- Drain most of the fat off (all but about a tablespoon) and then add the potatoes and sear until golden brown on the outside, about 10-15 minutes. When the potatoes are nicely browned, add the red pepper, carrots and onion and cook until the vegetables are soft.
- Stir in the flour until well blended. Then slowly add the chicken and veal stocks, stirring constantly until thickened. Simmer five minutes.
- Blend in the cheddar cheese and beer, stirring constantly until the cheese melts.
- Add the salt, pepper, cream, Tabasco, and Worcestershire Sauce. Let simmer for at least 30 minutes. Two hours of simmering will make for a much thicker, heartier soup. If you don't have the time to wait, you can thicken it up by running a cup or two of the soup through a blender and then adding the blended liquid back to the soup.
- To serve, garnish with some grated Parmesan cheese and some croutons or a potato pancake.

Roasted Acorn Squash Soup

Ingredients:

1 Med. or 2 Small Acorn Squash, peeled and roasted
2 Tbsp .... Olive Oil
To Taste .... Salt and Pepper
3 Tbsp .... Butter
2 .... Shallots, finely chopped
1 Tbsp .... Dried Thyme
1 Clove .... Garlic, minced
½ Cup .... White Wine
2 Cups .... Chicken Stock, (or a little more if too thick)
1 Cup .... Heavy Cream
.... Fresh Thyme for Garnish

Method:

- Pre-heat the oven to 400°. Peel the acorn squash, and cut into 1" to 2" pieces. Rub a little olive oil on the squash and season with salt and pepper to taste. Place on a sheet tray and roast for about 45 minutes or until lightly browned and caramelized. Remove from oven and reserve.
- Heat a 4-quart pan over medium heat.
- Add the butter and sweat the shallots until clear. Add the garlic and thyme and cook until fragrant. Raise the heat to high.
- Add the white wine and cook until reduced by 1/3.
- Add the chicken stock, the roasted acorn squash and the cream and cook until warmed through, about 10 to 15 minutes. Place the soup in a blender or food processor, or use a hand-held blender to puree the soup until smooth.
- Garnish with fresh thyme and serve. You can also top with a dollop of crème fraiche or sour cream.

Tips: This is a recipe that can be played with a lot. You can use pumpkin, yellow squash, or butternut squash in place of the acorn squash. If you want more of a pumpkin taste you can use pumpkin spice, or cinnamon and nutmeg. If you like something with a little kick, you can add cayenne pepper to taste. I would add the cayenne pepper with the thyme, so you get the full flavor. You could also use sherry instead of, or in conjunction with, the wine. Sherry works very well with any cream based soup. Another good tip is to use a little vinegar in any bean soup about 5 minutes before serving. The vinegar makes the bean taste pop in your mouth.

Roasted Chestnut Soup

Ingredients:
1 Lb.	Chestnuts
1 Tbsp	Butter
1 Large	Shallot, finely minced
1 Medium	Leek, finely minced
¼ Lb.	Mushrooms, diced
1 Tsp.	Salt
To Taste	Pepper
1 Clove	Garlic, minced
1 Tbsp	Fresh Parsley
2 ½ Cups	Water
2 ½ Cups	Chicken Stock
1 Tsp	Sugar
½ Cup	Heavy Cream

Method:
- Roast chestnuts, with shells on, in 350° oven until light brown, about 10 to 12 minutes. Let cool and remove the shells.
- In a 4-quart pan over medium heat, sweat the shallots, leeks and mushrooms in the butter until transparent, about 10 minutes. Add salt and pepper to taste.
- Add garlic and fresh parsley and stir. Add the roasted chestnuts.
- Add water, chicken sock, and sugar and simmer for 20 to 30 minutes.
- Place soup in blender and blend until smooth.
- Add the cream, cook for 5 minutes, taste, and adjust the seasonings.
- Serve with crusty warm bread.

Roasted Corn and Chorizo Soup

Ingredients:

3 Ears	Fresh Corn, fire roasted
1	Pablano Pepper, roasted
2 Tbsp	Olive Oil
1 Medium	White Onion, finely chopped
1	Red Pepper, cut into small dice
4	Aidells Smoked Chorizo Sausage links
1 Tbsp	Spanish Paprika
1 Tsp	Chipotle Powder
2 Tbsp	Mexican Oregano
1 Clove	Garlic, minced
2 to 3 Large	Potatoes, cut into ½" cubes
3 Tbsp	Fresh Cilantro, finely chopped
1	Bay Leaf
15 oz.	Canned, Crushed Tomatoes
1	Lime, cut in half
2 Cups	Homemade Chicken Stock
	Salt and Pepper

Method:

- Remove corn leaves and silk and roast corn over gas stove grate or on the grill, until the tips of the corn kernels have slightly blackened. Set aside to cool. After corn has cooled to the touch, slice the corn from the cob. Reserve the cobs.
- Roast the Pablano chili peppers until charred black and place into a bowl covered with plastic wrap to steam them. When cooled, remove and discard the skin and seeds and chop the pepper into a small dice.
- Heat a stockpot or Dutch oven over medium-high heat. Add olive oil.
- Add the onions, red pepper; and a pinch of salt and sauté until soft.
- Add the sausage and HALF of the spices and cook until fragrant.
- Add garlic, potatoes, and chopped roasted Pablano chili peppers.
- Add remaining spices, fresh cilantro, bay leaf, corn, and crushed tomatoes.
- Squeeze the lime into the pot and drop it in to cook.
- With the back of your knife, scrape the corn cobs to remove all the corn pulp and add to the pot. Drop the corn ears into the pot to cook with the other ingredients.
- Add chicken stock.
- Taste and adjust seasonings.
- Simmer and cook until potatoes are tender, about two hours.
- Remove the corn cobs and limes before serving.

Roasted Corn Chowder

Ingredients:

2 Ears	Corn
3 Tbsp	Butter
3 Tbsp	All Purpose Flour
2	Shallots, finely chopped
1 Clove	Garlic, minced
¼ Tsp	Cayenne pepper
2 Tsp	Thyme
1 Tsp	Whole Cumin Seeds, toasted and freshly ground
To Taste	Salt and Pepper
2 Cups	Chicken Stock, (or a little more if too thick)
1 Lg. or 2 Small	Potatoes, diced
1 Cup	Heavy Cream
3 Strips	Applewood Smoked Bacon, fried until crispy for garnish

Method:

- Start by shucking the corn and either grilling or roasting over an open flame on your gas stove. If you roast the corn on your stove, stay close by and keep an eye on the corn. You will need to turn the corn about every minute. The same holds true for grilling. When the corn is cooked, cut the kernels from the cob. Once the kernels have been cut, use the back of your knife (the spine) and scrape along the ear length wise to get every drop of corn goodness. This is called milking the corn.
- Heat a 4-quart pot over medium heat, add the butter and cook until the butter is melted and starting to turn brown. Add the flour and stir to form a paste (called a white roux.) Let cook 2 to 3 minutes to cook out the flour taste.
- Add the shallots and garlic and cook until the shallots are softened, about 4 to 5 minutes.
- Add the corn, cayenne pepper, thyme and cumin. Stir to combine. Add salt and pepper to taste. While stirring, slowly add the chicken stock.
- Bring to a simmer, add the potatoes and cook until the potatoes are soft.
- Add the cream and cook for 5 minutes before serving. Serve in bowls and top with crumbled bacon.

Tip: As I am writing this, I'm thinking that adding some grilled chicken on top of this would be tasty too.

Smoked Chicken Soup

Ingredients:

5	Chicken Thighs
1 Tbsp. + 1¼ Tsp.	Street Chef Poultry Seasoning (See the recipe in the 'Street Chef's Seasoning Mixtures' section of the book.)
½ Cup + a little	Peanut Oil
½ Cup	All-Purpose Flour
½ Small	Onion, diced
1 Large	Red Pepper, diced
3 Ears	Fresh Corn
3	Potatoes, diced
5	Carrots, diced
To Taste	Salt and Pepper
6 Cups	Chicken Stock
½ Bag	Dried Small Red Beans (½ of a 1 pound bag)
2	Chipotle Peppers in Adobo Sauce (You can make your own following the recipe in the 'Vegetable Recipes' section of the book or buy them canned in your favorite Latin market or large grocery store.)

Method:

- Season the chicken thighs with 1 tablespoon of the Poultry Seasoning, place the seasoned chicken in a smoker, and smoke for 1 hour.
- After 1 hour, remove the chicken from the smoker, slice it into small pieces, and sauté in a little oil in a pan over high heat.
- Heat ½ cup of oil in a Dutch oven. Add the flour and stir to make a roux. Cook the roux until it turns a light brown (peanut colored) and then add the onion and red pepper and season with a teaspoon of the Poultry Seasoning.
- Roast the 3 ears of corn by placing them on a grill, over the flame of a gas stove, or under the broiler. Let the corn cool and then cut the kernels from the cob. After the corn is cut from the cob, turn the knife over and use the dull end to scrape over the corn left on the cob to release the milky juices. This is also known as "milking" the cob.
- Cut the potatoes and carrots into a ¼" dice and season with salt and pepper and ¼ teaspoon of the Poultry Seasoning.
- Sauté the potatoes and carrots in the same pan that you used for the chicken. When they are nicely browned, add them to the roux, along with the chicken stock, corn, beans and Chipotles in Adobo sauce. Bring it all to a boil.
- Reduce the heat and simmer for 2 hours.

Tortilla Soup

(Serves 8)

Ingredients:

1 Tbsp.	Lard, Butter or Olive Oil
1 Med. or ½ Lrg	White Onion, finely chopped
To Taste	Salt and Pepper
1 Tsp.	Ground Cumin
1 Tsp.	Guajillo Chili Powder
2 Cloves	Garlic, minced
4 Cups	Homemade Chicken Stock
1 to 2	Tomatoes, peeled, seeded and cut into ½" dice
1 or 2	Chipotles in Adobo Sauce
10	Tortillas, cut into small dice
1 Cup	Water, if needed
¼ Cup	Cilantro, finely chopped
10	Tortillas cut into ¼" wide strips for garnish

Method:

- Heat a 4-quart saucepan over medium-high heat. Let the pan heat several minutes and then add the lard, butter or oil. Add onions, a good pinch of salt and sauté until tender, about 3 to 5 minutes.
- Add black pepper and half of the cumin and guajillo chili powder. Cook until fragrant. Add garlic and stir to incorporate.
- Add chicken stock, chopped tomatoes, chipotles in adobo sauce and the remaining cumin and guajillo powder. Add diced tortillas and stir to incorporate. Bring to a boil and reduce heat to a simmer.
- Cover and cook ½ hour, stirring occasionally. If it becomes too thick, add some water to thin. Add cilantro just before serving.
- Heat ½" of oil in sauté pan, or if you have a deep fryer all the better. Add tortilla strips and fry until crisp and golden brown. As soon as the tortillas come out of the oil, season with salt and a pinch of guajillo chili powder.
- Ladle soup into a bowl and top with fried tortilla strips to serve.

Tuscana Soup

Ingredients:

4 to 6	Italian Sausage links
1	Yellow Onion, finely chopped
2 Cloves	Garlic, minced
2 Large	Potatoes, cut into ½" cubes
To Taste	Red Pepper Flakes
To Taste	Salt and Pepper
Splash	White Wine to deglaze
5 to 6	Kale Leaves, chopped into bite-sized pieces
2 Cups	Chicken Stock
2 Cups	Heavy Cream

Method:

- Heat pan over medium-high heat. Sauté the sausage until almost cooked. Remove and slice.
- Lower the heat and sweat onions until clear.
- Add garlic and potatoes with HALF of the red pepper flakes, salt and pepper. Add a splash of white wine and cook until almost dry.
- Add kale and cook until slightly wilted.
- Add sliced sausages, chicken stock, cream and remaining red pepper flakes, if desired.
- Taste and adjust seasonings.
- Simmer and cook until potatoes are tender, about 1 hour.
- Taste again and adjust seasonings.

Tip: A shot of sherry is a nice addition to any cream based soup.

Knife Skills

One of the most important things in the kitchen is learning about your knives. The more you use your knives the more comfortable you will be using them and the faster and more proficient you will become. This will save you time and energy and result in more uniform cuts.

Each knife is used for a specific purpose and is described in detail in the following section. Get to know your knives and let them work for you. For instance, when using larger knives like the chef's knife, let the weight of the knife do some of the work for you. And treat your knives right. With proper care, they will last you a lifetime. Always use a cutting board made of wood, plastic, or composite material. Never, ever, use a glass or stone cutting board as they will take the edge off your knife that you have worked so hard to maintain. And always clean your knives after they have been used but never place them in the dishwasher or in the sink to soak. This is hard on the knives and dangerous as well. And speaking of safety, always store your knives in a sleeve, a knife block, or, if you're lucky enough to have the space in your kitchen, in a knife drawer designed just for them.

Construction of the Knife

Today there are many different types and brands of knives available. Until recently, all knives were made of high carbon steel, high carbon stainless steel or Titanium. Now there is also a ceramic blade available. Below are brief descriptions of the different materials used, including ceramic, to help you determine which is best for you.

High Carbon Steel

Knives made of high carbon steel hold an edge better than just about any other type of steel. High carbon steel requires less maintenance before and after each use because of the hardness of the steel. There are several drawbacks, however. Over time, the blade will discolor and eventually turn black. High carbon steel can also be prone to rust and some people say that the high carbon blades impart a metallic taste to the food. Since everyone's sense of taste is different, you'll have to judge that one for yourself. With proper care, such as cleaning, drying and storing in a block or knife guard, the knife will last a lifetime. An example of a high carbon steel knife would be a Sabatier Au Carbon.

High Carbon Stainless Steel

This type of knife is by far the most popular in use today. High carbon stainless steel has a high carbon content for hardness, but also has Chromium to keep it looking great. High carbon stainless steel will take a sharp edge and maintain it well, but it does require more frequent maintenance. European knives produce a softer, thicker blade and require less maintenance than the Japanese high carbon stainless steel. A good example of European knives would be Wusthof or Henckels. Japanese knives use an alloy and a heat treatment that produces harder, thinner steel, but they do require more maintenance than the European knives described above. Global or MAC knives are good examples of this type of steel construction.

Titanium

Titanium blades are actually a mix of titanium and carbides. Titanium is lighter than steel and more wear resistant. Titanium will hold an edge longer than steel. This type of construction is great for filleting or boning knives.

Ceramic

Ceramic is the newest type of knife construction. Ceramic knives are made up of a material called Zirconium oxide. The blades are extremely sharp and maintain an edge very well for months with little or no maintenance at all. They also impart no steel taste to the food. The two drawbacks to Ceramic knives are that they are brittle and come in limited sizes. Ceramic knives also require diamond-sharpening tools to maintain them and the tools are quite pricey. Ceramic knives should only be used on a cutting board because the ceramic is hard enough to cut the glaze on dinnerware.

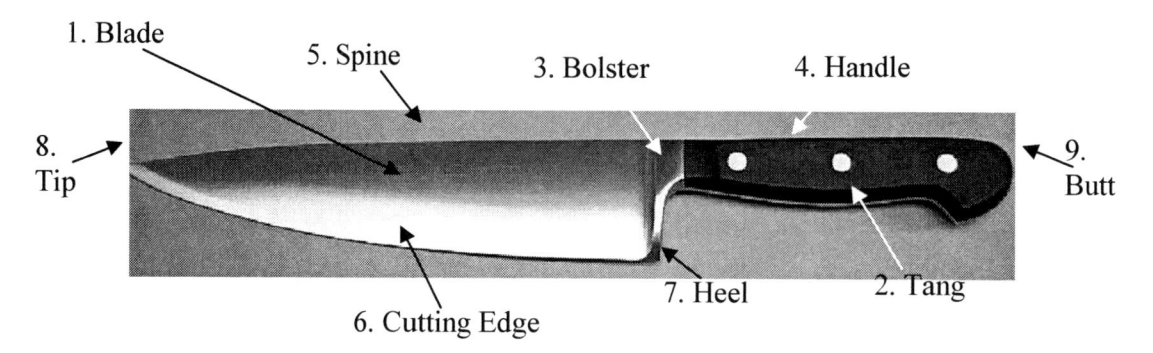

The parts that make up a knife are:
1. The blade
2. The tang (the part that goes into the handle. High-end knives have a full tang)
3. The bolster/finger guard
4. The handle
5. The spine
6. The cutting edge
7. The heel
8. The tip
9. The butt

Knife Production

Most metal knives are produced using either block or stamped steel from a blank and are then ground to shape. Block or stamped steel is a process where the metal is heated and then stamped into shape. High-end knives are forged. Forging produces a harder end product because the steel is heated and cooled several times. In forging, the blade is pounded into shape from a red-hot blank of steel. The final grinding and finishing are only cosmetic and superficial. Forging reduces impurities in the steel, which can contribute to the consistency of the metal from the front of the blade to the butt of the tang. Another advantage to forging is that the knife is made from a single piece of steel, bolster and all. Bolsters are found on the best quality chef knives and add rigidity, weight, safety, and improved balance. Wusthof and Sabatier knives are good examples of this type of construction. Henckels are not forged, but are built up by welding together the tang, bolster, and the blade.

Purchasing a Knife

There are many things to consider when selecting a knife or adding an additional knife to your set. Beyond selecting the right knife for the task at hand, you must consider the weight, handle size and handle type that is best for you. When selecting a knife, hold the knife in your hand. The knife should fit in your hand comfortably and should be well balanced. Even if you are going to order via the Internet, visit a retail store near you and try out the knives for heft and balance before placing your order. Handles vary in material and shape and come in wood, synthetic materials or metal. Some knives, such as Global, are metal from the tip to the butt. The final determining factor in which handle to choose is your preference and comfort with the style and fit.

Types of Knives and Their Uses

Knives are used to make basic cuts that are used everyday and in every recipe. As your knife skills improve, you will be able to do more complicated cuts and learn more advanced carving techniques. Part of your knife skills training includes choosing the proper knife for a given task.

Chef's Knife

A Chef's Knife is the workhorse of the kitchen and is usually 6" to 12" in length. This is the knife that you will use the vast majority of the time. The chef's knife can be used for meat as well as fruits and vegetables, and for tasks from slicing to chopping. A 6" knife is fine for smaller jobs, but if you are chopping a large quantity of food or cutting larger items, then a larger chef's knife may be a better choice.

Santuko Knife

Santuko Knives, which are used as a chef's knife, are usually 6" to 8" in length and have an unusual shape: The bottom edge is flat while the top edge curves down toward the tip. The blade is generally thinner than a chef's knife blade and, since Santuko knives do not have a bolster, they are not as heavy as a chef's knife. The Santuko is used for everything a chef's knife is used for. The choice between the two really comes down to personal preference.

Chef's Utility Knife

Chef's Utility Knives usually are 5" to 6" in length and are like mini chef's knifes. They basically do the same work as a chef's knife but are used for smaller jobs.

Boning Knife

Boning Knives are usually 5" to 6" in length and come in either a flexible blade or a stiff blade. Flexible knifes are best used on fowl and fish and the stiffer blades are used for beef, lamb, pork and other meats.

Paring Knife

Paring Knives are generally 2" to 5" in length and are designed for doing smaller jobs. The blade generally has a smaller profile, which is great for separating citrus segments or melon slices. The slimmer profile of the paring knife blade helps keep food from sticking to the blade. The paring knife's main uses include peeling and carving fruits and vegetables.

Bird's Beak Knife

Bird's Beak Knives are generally 2" in length and are designed for creating tourne (barrel shapes), vegetable carving, and vegetable peeling. The blade has a slight curve and resembles a bird's beak, thus the name.

Slicing Knife

Slicing Knives are typically 6" to 12" in length and come in both a round tip and a pointed tip. Slicers are usually fairly flexible knives. Round tips are used for slicing large pieces of meat and fish without bones. The pointed tip is better suited for slicing poultry or fowl where there are a fair amount of bones to carve around.

Serrated Slicing Knife

Serrated Slicing Knives are typically 6" to 10" in length and are excellent for cutting bread, tomatoes and pineapples.

Fillet Knife

Fillet Knives are typically 6" to 12" in length and generally have narrow and flexible blades that are designed for filleting fish.

Cleavers

Cleavers are larger knives used to cut through bones and to deal with heavy-duty meat cutting and chopping applications.

Types of Edges

Flat Ground

The blade profile tapers from the thicker spine to the thinner edge in a straight or convex line. They are heavier and tougher than the hollow ground blades, which have a concave profile. This type of edge can be sharpened.

Serrations

Serrations are wavy types of blades and are best used for slicing softer materials like breads, fruits, and vegetables. Serrated knives are used in a sawing motion and cannot be sharpened.

Granton Edge

These types of knives have oval areas ground in to the side of the knife. The ovals are ground into one or both sides of the blade to help keep food from sticking to the blade.

Sharpening and Steeling

Knife blade angles for sharpening

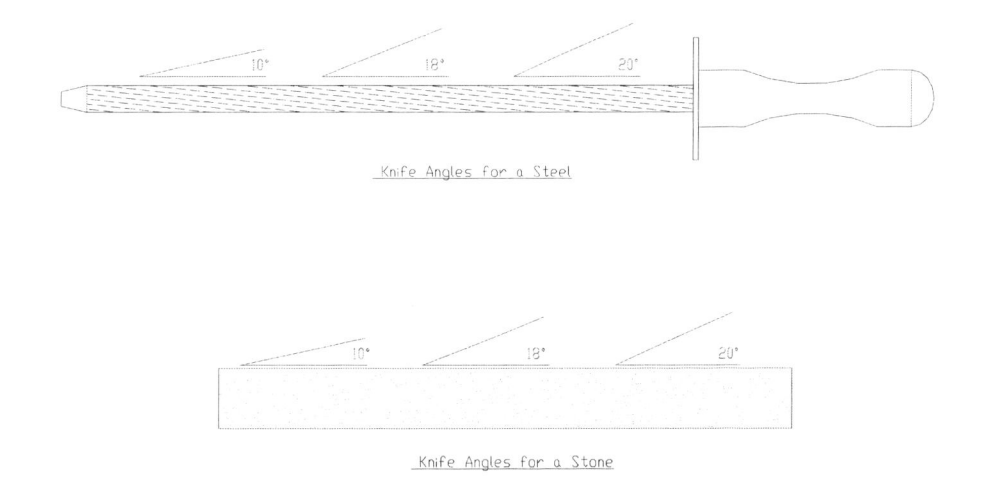

Knife Angles for a Steel

Knife Angles for a Stone

Method for Using a Wet Stone

If your knife has not been sharpened for a while, it is best to start with a wet stone. A wet stone is simply a stone that is either soaked in water, or that has had oil applied to it. I would recommend using water rather than oil. Starting with the heel of the knife at an 18 to 20 degree angle, or a 10 degree angle if sharpening a Global knife or any of the other high end Japanese knives, pull the knife across the stone from the heel to the tip. Flip the knife and pull the knife across the stone at the same angle in the same direction. Always do an even number of strokes on both sides. This is critical, as you want the blade to be even. As you do this, look at the knife-edge closely to see if there are any chips in the knife blade. A lot of stones have 2 sides, a coarse side and a fine side. If the knife blade is in bad shape, start with the coarse side and finish with the fine side. Keep working the knife on the stone until all spots are gone and the blade has a smooth edge. After you have finished with the stone, you will need to steel the knife. The steel is very fine and is used after the stone to align the blade and remove any burrs from the stone. It's like working with different grades of sand paper.

Method for Using a Steel

If your knife is in relativity good shape, you should only have to steel the blade before or after each use. This keeps the blade edge in alignment. Starting with the heel of the knife at an 18 to 20 degree angle, pull the knife across the steel from the heel to the tip. Flip the knife and pull the knife across the steel at the same angle in the same direction. Always do an even number of strokes on both sides. This is critical, as you want the blade to be even.

Holding the Knife

For chef's knives and Santuko type knives, grip the handle with three fingers, resting the index finger on one side of the blade and holding the thumb on the opposite side of the blade. This adds stability and helps keep the blade from twisting from side to side. For smaller knifes grip the handle with all fingers. Always handle the knife with respect, as it is sharp and be aware of protecting the guiding hand, which is the hand not holding the knife. The guiding hand guides the object being cut, prevents slippage, and helps control the cut size. The fingertips of the guiding hand should hold the object with the thumb held back from the fingertips. The fingertips should also be tucked under slightly, with the knife blade resting against the knuckles of the "guiding hand", preventing the fingers from being cut.

Basic Culinary Cuts

All of the cuts listed below are standard culinary cuts throughout the world. Just about every culture uses one or more of the cuts below. Whether you are working in a professional kitchen or cooking for friends and family, learning how to correctly master these cuts will help improve your cooking and the final presentation of your food. Cooking vegetables that are cut uniformly will result in food that is cooked evenly. Different sized cuts can be used for foods that vary in cooking time. A large dice takes longer to cook than a brunoise, so consider this when you are preparing a recipe.

To make all of the cuts listed below, create a flat surface to work from. Start by slicing a round edge off the vegetable lengthwise so you have a flat surface to work with. Next, place the cut side down and slice the next side of the vegetable and repeat until you have leveled all four sides. Now slice the ends to finish off your rectangle. For julienne cuts, slice the rectangle to create 2½" lengths, and then slice the 2½" lengths into 1/8" sections. At this point you will have a series of rectangles 2½" long and 1/8" thick. Now slice the rectangles lengthwise into 1/8" strips. Now you have julienne cut vegetables. To make brunoise, stack the julienne strips, rotate, and cut to make 1/8" squares. This same principal is used for all cuts listed below.

The Basic Cuts Include:
    Large Dice ¾"x ¾"x ¾"
    Medium Dice ½"x ½"x ½"
    Small Dice ¼"x ¼"x ¼"
    Brunoise 1/8"x 1/8"x1/8"
    Fine Brunoise 1/16"x 1/16" x 1/16"
    Batonnet ¼"x ¼"x 2½" to 3"
    Julienne 1/8" x 1/8" x 2½"
    Fine Julienne 1/16"x 1/16" x 2½"
    Alumette 1/8"x 1/8"x 2½" (alumette refers only to potatoes)

Chiffonade/Shredding

The chiffonade cut is used for leafy herbs and vegetables. The result is a finely shredded product, often used as a garnish or bed. The method is as follows:

Herbs such as basil and sage are good choices to chiffonade. Stack the leaves on top of each other and roll up into a tight cylinder. Make very fine cuts, cutting across the cylinder to produce fine shreds.

Shredding is used for greens, lettuces, cabbage or Belgian endive. Start by removing the core of the lettuce. Slice the lettuce lengthwise in half, working with one half at a time, slice the half head lengthwise. Rotate the lettuce and make 1/8" cuts. Repeat the same for the other half. If you would like wider strips, cut into ¼" to 1" slices.

Cutting Onions and Shallots

Onions and shallots grow in layers and require a slightly different technique than more solid foods. The technique is as follows:

If you are right handed, place the onion on its side with the root end pointing to the left and the top pointing to the right. Holding the onion with your left hand, use your chef's knife to slice the top off. This will give you a flat surface to work with. Working with a flat surface is always best. Place the cut side or the top of the onion on the cutting board and slice through the root end to cut the onion in half. Now remove the outer brown layers of skin to reveal the white part of the onion. Lay the onion cut-side down and make a series of vertical cuts from just before the root end out to the top of the onion. Be careful not to slice through the root end, as this is what holds the onion together. If you want fine cut onions, you will need to make your cuts close together. Likewise if you want a large dice, then the cuts will be spaced farther apart. This is the way to achieve a cut from minced to large dice. Now make 2 to 3 horizontal cuts from the front back to the root end. Again, do not cut all the way through the onion. Now, turn the onion and slice down through it, making even crosswise cuts. The closer the cuts are together, the finer the dice will be. When you are finished cutting the onion, there should be a small root end left that is just about the size of a quarter.

Other Cuts

Paysanne (Pronounced pay-zahn which means peasant). Paysanne cut vegetables can be cut and sliced into squares, circles, triangles, or half rounds. All are cut thinly (1/8 " thick) and about ½" wide.

Fermiere (Pronounced fair-me-a, which means Farmer). Fermiere cut vegetables are cut into round discs or small squares resembling Scrabble tiles. Although size may vary, 1" squares that are ¼ " thick are customary.

Losange (Pronounced low-songe). Losange cut vegetables are diamond shaped cuts. Slice your vegetables or fruit 1/8" thick and ½" wide. Cut the slice on the bias every ½" to create diamond shapes.

Decorative Cuts

Tourne

These are barrel or football shaped pieces. They are 2" long x ¾" in diameter with 7 sides. Begin by cutting the vegetable into a rectangle ¾" x ¾" x 2" long. Make a cut from slightly off center from one end to the other lengthwise curving out towards the middle and then back to slightly off center on the opposite side. The cut should look like the long side of a football. Rotate and continue cutting each edge until a football shape is achieved.

Fluting

Fluting is a decorative cut used on mushrooms. Hold the mushroom between the thumb and fingers. Place the blade at an angle against the mushroom cap center. Rest the thumb of the cutting hand on the mushroom to brace it. Rotate the knife toward the cap edge to cut a shallow groove. At the same time the knife is cutting, turn the mushroom in the opposite direction. This will take some practice, but is a really nice looking way to do mushrooms.

Other Knife Techniques

Garlic Paste

Garlic paste is used for salad dressings and for other dishes where you want the taste of garlic without the bits. Garlic is purchased in heads and within the head are cloves. You start by removing a clove from the head and placing it on a cutting board. Place the side of your knife flat on top of the clove with the blade edge pointing away from you and give it a whack. This will slightly crush the clove making it easier to remove the outer skin. Peel and slice the garlic. Then rotate the slices and mince the garlic. Place the minced garlic in a pile and sprinkle with coarse salt. The coarse salt acts as an abrasive and will draw the moisture out of the garlic. Place the side of the knife on top of the pile of garlic with the blade edge pointing away from you and, while pushing the knife down firmly, pull the knife towards you through the pile of garlic. Repeat this process until you attain the desired consistency.

How to Choose a Steak

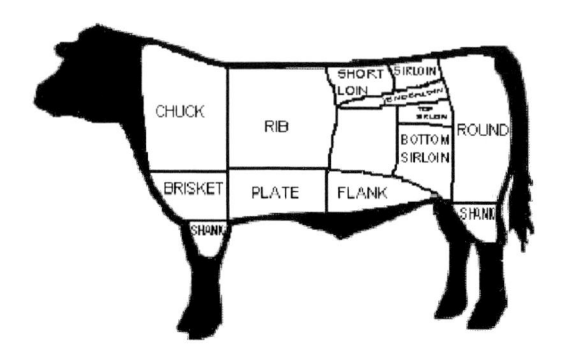

Buying Steak

Most beef available in the market and labeled 'steak', is good for grilling, with some of the tenderest and tastiest cuts also being the most expensive. Look for a steak that has good 'marbling', the white fat that runs evenly throughout the meat. Fat is where the flavor comes from. A well-marbled steak offers more flavor than leaner cuts and stays juicy and tender during cooking. Get to know your local butcher. Butchers generally have higher quality meats and many can offer to age the meat for you. Aging is a process where the meat is placed in a meat locker and allowed to sit for 30 to 40 days. This is also known as a hanger steak. In the aging process, the outer part of the meat dries out and flavors intensify. At the end of the aging process, the dried meat is trimmed away and discarded. The additional time required and the loss of meat are why an aged steak is so much more expensive. The meat itself should be a deep red color, indicating a well-aged and tender cut of beef. Avoid meats that are brown and reduced for quick sale. The best cuts of meat for grilling are from the areas where the muscles are used the least, such as from the back of the animal, and include the rib and loin sections. Cuts from the muscles that are used a lot, such as round, chuck, and shank, are best suited for longer cooking times, such as braising, stewing and low heat barbequing.

Steaks cut 1" thick are ideal for the grill. Below are the most common cuts available at your local grocery store or butcher.

Tenderloin
: This boneless elongated muscle is lean and the tenderest cut of beef. (Includes the short loin and top loin

Porterhouse
: This cut has the bone in and includes portions of both the tenderloin (more) and top loin (less). This is one of the most flavorful steaks.

T-bone
: This cut is similar to a porterhouse, has a T-shaped bone and includes portions of top loin (more) and tenderloin (less).

Sirloin
: Found between the short loin and round, this cut is tender and has good flavor. The top sirloin is the tenderest of the sirloin cuts.

New York Strip (Kansas City, Delmonico)
: Known by many names, this cut from the top loin has good flavor. With the bone in, it's known as a club steak.

Rib or Rib Eye
: Cut from the rib section, the rib eye is very flavorful and the name is the same with the bone removed.

Flank Steak
: Flank steak is ideal for marinating. The meat should be cooked over high heat to form a crust on the outside and seal the meat juices on the inside. When done, the meat should be sliced very thinly on an angle against the grain for increased tenderness.

Prepping the Steak

Remove the steak from the refrigerator and place on the countertop for 20 minutes, plated and covered with plastic wrap. This allows the steak, when cooked, to get sufficiently warmed at the center without any cold spots. This is an especially important step if you like your steak served rare. For a tenderloin or filet mignon, which has very little fat, brush both sides with a canola or other neutral tasting high heat oil to keep it from sticking to the grill. For added flavor use a spice rub or marinade. For all steaks, prior to grilling, pat dry with paper towels. That includes steak that's been marinated.

Grilling Steak

Have your grill fired-up to high heat, which means that you can only stand to hold your hand over the flame for about two seconds. Place the steak directly over the flame of a high heat fire. The high heat seals the steak's surface and helps seal in those flavorful meat juices. Leave for three minutes. Do not attempt to move the steak, as it will most likely stick to the grill. Once the surface of the meat caramelizes, the protein structure will change and the meat will release itself from the grill. Turn the steak over and grill for another three minutes. Turn the steak again and rotate ¼ turn, cooking one minute more on each side for rare. If you like your steak more done, move it to a cooler part of the grill to finish cooking. Meat will continue to cook after it has been removed from the grill from the residual heat within the steak, so remove the meat from the heat about 5 to 8 degrees before it reaches the desired temperature and allow it to rest. The resting time will finish the cooking. Use an instant-read thermometer inserted into the center of the meat to check for doneness.

If you don't have a grill, try pan-searing and oven-roasting your steak.

Pan-Seared and Oven-Roasted Steak

Pre-heat the oven to 375°. Place the sauté pan or cast iron skillet over high heat. Let the pan heat for several minutes until the pan is hot. Season the steak with salt and pepper or your favorite spice mixture. Place the steak into the hot pan to sear the steak's surface and seal in those flavorful meat juices. Leave for two to three minutes. Do not attempt to move the steak, as it will most likely stick to the pan. Once the surface of the meat caramelizes, the protein structure will change and the meat will release itself from the grill. Turn the steak over and cook for another minute. Place in the oven for 3 to 8 minutes until cooked to desired doneness. The residual heat within the steak will continue to cook the meat after it has been removed from the pan, so remove the meat from the heat about 5 to 8 degrees before it reaches the desired temperature and allow it to rest.

Suggested Temperatures

- Rare- 125° F
- Med. Rare- 135° F
- Medium- 145° F
- Well done- 165° F

Serving

Let the steak stand 10 minutes per pound before cutting. This allows all those good juices to redistribute throughout the meat. A pat of unsalted fresh butter melted on top adds a beautiful sheen and a depth of flavor, but is not required.

Choosing Other Cuts of Beef

Chuck
This cut is used for things like pot roast and stews and is ground for hamburgers. When ground, this is by far the most flavorful for meat loafs, hamburgers and Salisbury steak. When choosing a chuck steak, look for a well-marbled steak without excessive fat. A properly trimmed steak should have no more than a ¼" of fat around the outside.

Shank
Shanks are primarily used for braising and stew-like dishes. The shanks are seared under high heat to seal the juices in and then braised or placed in a stew and cooked until the meat is almost falling off the bone.

Brisket
Brisket is used for corned beef and for beef barbeque. Once again, the meat is cooked at low heat for long periods. Barbeque lovers use this cut for its flavor.

Flank Steak
Flank steak is a little different from other cuts of meats. The flank steak or London broil cut, lends itself to marinating and grilling. The meat does not have a lot of flavor by itself, but marinating it will add a lot of flavor. The cut is a grainy cut and must be trimmed against the grain to insure tenderness. If the steak is cut with the grain, it will be very tough.

Plate Cut
Also known as skirt steak, the plate cut, is a cut just below the flank steak and is generally somewhat fatty. This is why it is so flavorful. This cut is primarily smoked and cooked for longer periods. The cut is great for doing smoked skirt steak tacos.

Basic Cuts of Lamb

The basic cuts of lamb are:

Shoulder
Shoulder roast, boneless lamb shoulder chops, and ground shoulder.

Rack
Rack of lamb (can be Frenched – the fat and meat are trimmed from between the ribs and the bones are scraped clean creating that distinctive look of the rack with individual bones protruding from it), lamb rib chops.

Loin
Lamb loin, boneless saddle of lamb (double loin roast), lamb loin chops.

Leg
Leg of lamb (either bone-in or bone-out), Boneless Baron of lamb (double striploin, rump and leg area of a full carcass - in other words, the entire rear half of a lamb carcass.).

Shank
Lamb shank (shin portion of the fore or hind legs).

Breast
Boneless breast, Denver ribs.

Beef, Veal, and Pork Recipes

Cajun Empanadas

(Makes about 20 Empanadas)

Ingredients:

2 Medium	Baking Potatoes, cut into ¼" dice
1 Tbsp	Olive Oil
1 Pkg.	Andouille Sausage, about 1 Lb.
1 Medium	Onion, finely chopped
1 Clove	Garlic, finely minced
2 Stalks	Celery, finely chopped
1 Medium	Red Bell Pepper, cut into ¼" dice
½ Cup	Chicken Stock or Veal Stock
1 Tbsp	Hot Sauce
2 Tbsp	Tomato Paste
Double Recipe	Empanada Pastry (or package of pre-made Empanada wrappers)
	Vegetable Oil for Frying

Seasoning Mix

½ Tsp	Paprika
½ Tsp	Cayenne Pepper
½ Tsp	Onion Powder
¼ Tsp	Garlic Powder
½ Tsp	Dry Mustard
1 Tsp	Black Pepper
1 Tsp	Dried Oregano
½ Tsp	Dried Thyme
1 Tsp	Salt

Method:

- Mix all the herbs and spices for the seasoning mix together, place in a small bowl, and reserve.
- In a 4-quart pan, add the potatoes and cover with water. Cook about 20 minutes, until almost cooked. The potatoes should still have a little resistance. Remove from the heat, drain and place in cold water to cool.
- Heat a 4-quart sauté pan over high heat for several minutes. Add the olive oil and the sausage and cook until slightly caramelized. Remove from the pan and let cool.
- Add the onions, garlic, celery, and bell pepper to the pan and cook until softened and slightly caramelized.
- Add half of the seasoning mixture, stir, and cook until it starts to stick to the pan.
- Add the potatoes and the remaining seasoning mixture. Stir to combine, being careful not to break up the potatoes. Cook until blended.

- Add the chicken stock, hot sauce, and tomato paste. Mix to combine and cook for 5 minutes. Remove from the heat and let cool.
- To prepare the Empanadas, either roll out a 6" circle of homemade dough or use a pre-made wrapper. Add several tablespoons of filling and fold in half to make a half circle. Crimp the edges together using a fork. Place on a sheet pan (do not let them touch) and place in the refrigerator until ready to cook.
- To cook, heat a deep fryer or a Dutch oven filled 1/3 with vegetable oil to 350°. Place several empanadas in the oil at a time and cook until golden brown, about 3 to 5 minutes. Serve hot.

Tip: This is another dish that you can have a lot of fun with. These can be filled with so many things: eggs, bacon, and cheese; mini meatballs, tomato sauce and mozzarella cheese; leftover ground pot roast and roasted potatoes to make an English miners pie…the possibilities are endless.

Carne Asada
(Serves 8)

Ingredients:

1 - 16 oz	Skirt Steak or London Broil ½" to ¾" thick
2-3 Tbsp	Tequila
Juice of 2	Limes
Zest of 1	Lime
1 to 2 Tbsp	Olive Oil
2 Tsp	Oregano
1 Tbsp	Ground Cumin
2 Tsp	Ground Ancho Chili Powder
To Taste	Salt and Pepper
2-3 Tbsp	Oil
1 Each	White Onion, Jalapeños, and Green and Red Peppers, sliced
2 Tbsp	Cilantro, chopped

Method:

- Marinate the steak in the tequila, lime juice, lime zest, olive oil, oregano and half of the cumin and chili powder. Marinate for at least 1 hour. Remove from marinade, pat dry with a paper towel, and season with remaining cumin, chili powder, salt and pepper.
- Heat a sauté pan over high heat for several minutes. Add oil to the pan and sauté the vegetables until tender. Remove and keep warm in the oven.
- Let the pan heat up again until hot. Sear the steak about 1 to 2 minutes per side depending on desired doneness. Remove steak and let rest for 5 minutes.
- If you have access to a grill, grill the steak with mesquite charcoal or smoke in a smoker with mesquite wood and finish on the grill. It is best served medium rare.
- If you have pan-seared the steak, return the vegetables to the pan to pick up the flavors of the steak.

Tip: Carne Asada can be served as a steak or sliced and served with frijoles, grilled vegetables, cilantro, cheese and salsa or hot sauce, all wrapped in a warm flour tortilla.

Hungarian Goulash

Ingredients:

2 Tbsp	Butter or Olive Oil
1 Large	Yellow Onion, cut into a fine dice
To Taste	Salt and Pepper
1½ to 2 Lbs.	Stewing Beef
¼ Cup	Red Wine
1 Small Can	Tomato Paste
3 Tbsp	Hungarian Paprika
	Water to cover the meat

Method:

- Heat a Dutch oven over medium heat. Add butter or olive oil and onions and sweat until soft. Remove the onions and set aside.
- Raise the heat to medium-high.
- While the Dutch oven is heating up, salt and pepper the stewing beef. When the pot is pre-heated, add about 10 to 15 pieces of the beef to the pot. If you add it all at the same time, the meat will steam. What we are looking for here are nicely browned pieces of meat. As each portion of meat is cooked, remove and set aside.
- When all the beef is done, deglaze the pan with the red wine and reduce by 2/3.
- Add the tomato paste and 1 tablespoon of paprika and cook for 5 minutes
- Add the sautéed onions and the seared beef and stir to coat. Add the remaining paprika and stir.
- Add enough water to cover the meat and bring to a boil. Reduce the heat and simmer about 2 hours or until thickened.
- Serve over cooked white rice. Some people really like serving it over noodles, but my Uncle Julian always served it over rice.

Meatloaf for Sandwiches

Ingredients:

1 Medium	Shallot, finely chopped
To Taste	Salt and Pepper
½ Lb.	Ground Veal
½ Lb.	Ground Pork
1 Tsp	Fennel Seed
1 Tsp	Ancho Chili Powder
1 Tbsp.	Herbs de Provence
¼ Tsp	Cayenne Pepper
1	Egg, slightly beaten
2 Slices	Whole Wheat Bread, crusts trimmed off, dampened with water
¼ Cup	Parmesan Cheese, freshly grated

Method:
- Heat pan over medium-high heat. Add the shallots, salt, and pepper, and cook until tender. Remove from the heat and let cool.
- Pre-heat the oven to 375°.
- In a bowl, add the ground meats and the remaining ingredients. Mix to combine into a ball.
- Lightly oil a sheet pan. Form the ball of meatloaf into a square, 6" long by 4" wide and 2" thick.
- Place in a pre-heated oven and cook about 40 minutes, or until an internal temperature of 140° is reached. Remove from the oven and sprinkle with some additional herbs De Provence.
- Let cool and slice into ½" thick pieces to make sandwiches.

Tip: This is a meatloaf I like to make just for sandwiches, but of course this could be used for dinner or lunch. Serve with roasted potatoes and corn or green beans.

Mechado ala Marie - A Typical Filipino Dish

(Serves 6 to 8)

Ingredients:

3 Lbs.	Beef Brisket, sliced into 1" by 1½" slices
1 - 1½ Lbs.	Pork, sliced into 1" by 1½" slices
1 Cup	Soy Sauce
½ Cup	Palm Vinegar (available at your local Asian market)
1 Large	Onion, finely diced
3 to 4	Bay Leaves
15	Cherry Tomatoes or 25 to 30 Grapes Tomatoes, sliced in half
1 Tbsp	Coarsely Cracked Black Peppercorns
4	Carrots, cut into 1" cubes
½ Cup	Achuette or Aannatto Seed Water (soak 1 Tbsp of seeds in half cup of boiling water (let soak the day before). Achuette is available at Latin and Asian markets and is used for flavor and color.
About 2-3 Cups	Chicken Stock, enough to cover the meat
2 to 3 Large	Potatoes, cut into 1" cubes

Method:

- Slice the meat and place in a bowl. Pour the soy sauce and vinegar over the meat. Add the onions, bay leaves, tomatoes, and cracked peppercorns to the bowl and let marinate for at least 3 hours, or better yet, overnight.
- Heat a Dutch oven over high heat. Remove the meat from the marinade and add to the pan in small batches, searing until nicely browned.
- Continue cooking in small batches until all the meat has been cooked. Strain the marinade thru a strainer and reserve the marinade.
- Place a small amount of oil in the Dutch oven and place the strained ingredients in the pan, cooking until softened. Add the seared meat, remaining marinade, and Annatto seed water into the pot. (Discard the seeds.) Bring the pot to a boil, then reduce the heat to a simmer.
- Add the carrots and cook until the stew becomes thickened.
- In a separate pan, heat a tablespoon of olive oil over medium heat, then add the potatoes and season with salt and pepper. Fry the potatoes until crisp on the outside and fluffy on the inside.
- Serve with rice. Spoon the potatoes over the rice and pour the stew on top. This is a wonderful dish for cold nights.

Negimaki

Ingredients:

¼ Cup	Sherry
¼ Cup	Rice Wine Vinegar
3 Tbsp	Soy Sauce
1 Tbsp	Sugar
1 Tsp	White Pepper
1 Tbsp	Vegetable Oil
¾ Lb.	Flank Steak
4 Bunches	Spring Onions

Method:

- In a shallow dish large enough to hold the flank steak, pour in the sherry, rice wine vinegar, soy sauce, sugar, white pepper and oil. Stir well to combine ingredients. Place the flank steak in the marinade and turn to coat both sides. Let the steak marinate in the refrigerator for at least 3 hours or, better yet, overnight.
- After the meat has finished marinating, drain the marinade and reserve.
- Grill the flank steak over a charcoal grill until medium rare. Remove the steak from the grill and let cool.
- Slice the flank steak in thin strips across the grain and reserve.
- Place the marinade in a small pot over medium heat and cook until it reduces to a glaze. About 10 to 15 minutes.
- Prepare an ice bath in a bowl and set aside.
- Fill a 4-quart pot with water and place on the stove over high heat. Bring to a boil.
- Clean the spring onions, removing the roots. Cut the spring onions into 3" long pieces.
- In batches, add the spring onions to the boiling water and blanch for about 2 minutes. Remove and place in an ice bath to cool and stop the cooking process. This will also set the color.
- Remove the spring onions from the water and pat dry. Place 3 spring onions together and wrap them with a piece of the medium rare flank steak, leaving the ends of the spring onions sticking out on both sides.
- Drizzle the reserved, reduced marinade glaze over the meat before serving.

New Shepherds Pie

Ingredients:

2 Tbsp	Olive Oil
1 Medium	Onion, finely chopped
½ Lb.	Lamb Shoulder
2/3 Cup	Beef Stock
¾ Lb.	Sirloin Steak
To Taste	Salt
1/8 Tsp	Cayenne Pepper
½ Tsp	Freshly Ground Black Pepper
¼ Tsp	White Pepper
1 Tbsp	Fresh Parsley, chopped
½ Cup	Beaujolais or Other Red Wine
2 Tbsp	Bisto Gravy Mix (this is available at many supermarkets)
4 Medium	Baking Potatoes
¾ Cup	Heavy Cream
2 Tbsp	Butter
1	Pie Crust
½ Tsp	Paprika

Method:

- Pre-heat a sauté pan over medium-high heat. Add olive oil and sauté the onions until soft. Remove and set a side.
- Trim the lamb meat from the bones and add the bones to the stock and let simmer until the stock is needed.
- Cut the sirloin and lamb into ½" cubes. Re-heat the same pan you sautéed the onions in. Season the lamb and sirloin with salt and a combination of the three peppers, add a little olive oil to the pan and sear the meat over medium-high heat. Cook about 10 to 15 pieces at a time to avoid steaming the meat. What we are looking for here are nicely browned pieces of meat. As each portion of the meat is cooked, remove and set aside.
- When you finish cooking the meat, deglaze the pan with the red wine and reduce by half. Add the stock and bring to a boil.
- Mix the bisto into a small amount of water (about 4 tablespoons) and add the bisto mixture to the pan.
- Add the meat to the pan and let cook several minutes or until thickened. Then add the chopped fresh parsley.
- With the baking potatoes, cream, and butter, make mashed potatoes (see recipe in the Potatoes and Tubers section of this book.)
- Spread a pie crust into an oval tureen, add meat mixture, top with mashed potatoes, and sprinkle with paprika.
- Bake in a 350° oven until the potatoes are golden brown.

Osso Bucco

Ingredients:
- 1 to 2 Tbsp. .... Olive Oil
- To Taste .... Salt and Pepper
- 4 .... Veal Shanks
- 1 Medium .... Yellow Onion, diced
- 2 Cloves .... Garlic, minced
- 1 Tbsp. .... Basil, Thyme, Oregano or Marjoram (it's really a matter of taste)
- 1 Tsp. .... Red Pepper Flakes (optional or more if you like the sauce spicy)
- 2 Large .... Carrots, cut into ½" cubes
- 1 Stalk .... Celery, cut into ¼" pieces
- 1 Tbsp. .... Non-flavored Tomato Paste
- 1 Cup .... Red Wine
- 1 Cup .... Veal or Chicken Stock
- 1 .... Bay Leaf
- 1 - 28 oz. Can .... Good Quality Italian Whole Tomatoes

Method:
- Place a 5-quart sauté pan over medium-high heat and add the olive oil.
- Salt and pepper the veal shanks and sear on both sides until nicely browned. Remove the veal from the pan and set aside.
- Lower the heat to medium and sauté the onions and garlic until tender, being careful not to burn them. Add HALF of the dried herbs and the carrots and celery and cook about 5 minutes. Add the tomato paste and cook until dark red.
- Deglaze with red wine and cook until nearly dry. Add the veal stock and stir until incorporated. Add the remaining dried herbs and bay leaf.
- Crush the tomatoes with your hands and add to the heated pot. Bring to a slow simmer, taste, and adjust the seasonings.
- Add the veal shanks into the pan of sauce, cover and place into a heated 350° oven. Braise for 1 hour or until tender. Taste again and adjust the seasonings.
- To Serve: Place a veal shank in the middle of the plate and spoon the sauce on top. Serve with crusty bread and a nice red wine.

Pork Chops with Caramelized Onion Pan Gravy

Ingredients:

4 Tbsp.	Butter
2 Tbsp	Olive Oil
To Taste	Salt and Pepper
6	Bone-in Pork Chops, ¾" to 1" thick
1	Onion, cut in half and sliced thin
2 to 3 Cloves	Garlic, minced (optional)
1 to 2 Tbsp	Flour
1 Tsp	Oregano
¾ to 1 Cup	Milk

Method:

- Let a heavy-bottomed sauté pan pre-heat for 4 to 5 minutes. Add 1 tablespoon of butter and 2 tablespoons of olive oil and let the mixture heat until the butter starts to foam.
- Pre-heat the oven to 400°.
- Salt and pepper the pork chops, add them to the pan and sauté for 3 to 4 minutes on each side. Remove them from the pan and place in the oven to finish cooking, about 5 to 6 minutes.
- In the same pan that the pork chops were cooked in, add the remaining butter and heat over medium heat until it starts to foam.
- Add the sliced onions and cook for 10 to 15 minutes until caramelized. After about 5-8 minutes, add the garlic. The onions will cook way down and will turn brown and become sweet, not black and burnt. The garlic should turn a golden color.
- Raise the heat to medium-high and add the flour to the onion mixture, and cook stirring constantly for a full 3 minutes. The flour and butter mixture should be a light brown or peanut butter color.
- Add the oregano and let cook 1 minute.
- Slowly add cold milk to the pan with the onions and flour, stirring constantly. The mixture will thicken. Keep stirring and adding milk until the mixture is smooth. If it is too thick, add a little more milk and stir.
- Taste the gravy and add salt and pepper if needed.
- Remove the pork chops from the oven and place them in the caramelized onion gravy to coat. Sprinkle a little oregano on top to garnish
- Serve with mashed potatoes or pan-fried potatoes.

Sausages in Grape Sauce

Ingredients:
2	Italian Sausages
10 to 12	Seedless Grapes
¼ Cup	Balsamic Vinegar
1 to 2 Tbsp.	Butter

Method:
- Place the sausages in a baking dish, cover with the grapes, and sprinkle with the balsamic vinegar.
- Bake in the oven at 450° - 500° until the sausages are evenly browned, about 10 to 15 minutes.
- Remove the dish from the oven, let cool slightly.
- Stir the butter into the dish to make a sauce and serve.

Lamb Recipes

Lamb Kabobs

Ingredients:
½ Lb. .... Lamb Shoulder, cut into cubes about 2" square
.... Cherry Tomatoes
.... Cremini Mushrooms
.... Wooden Skewers

Marinade
¼ Cup .... Olive Oil
Zest of 1 .... Lemon
Juice of 1 .... Lemon
2 Tbsp. .... Fresh Oregano, finely chopped
To Taste .... Pepper

Method:
- Marinate the meat, tomatoes and mushrooms in half the marinade for 2 to 4 hours.
- While the meat is marinating, soak the wooden skewers in water.
- After marinating, place the meat, tomatoes, and mushrooms on the skewers. In a grill pan or charcoal grill over high heat, cook the kabobs turning once until desired doneness is achieved - about 3 to 5 minutes per side.
- Serve over cooked barley, rice or couscous. Drizzle the remaining unused marinade and a little fresh parsley over the lamb kabobs before serving.

Merguez Kefta

Ingredients:

2 Strips	Bacon, finely chopped
¼ Lb.	Ground Lamb
To Taste	Salt and Pepper
1 Small	Garlic Clove, finely chopped
¼ Tsp.	Cayenne Pepper
¼ Tsp.	Raz al Hanout (See recipe in the 'Street Chef's Seasoning Mixtures' section of the book.)
¼ Tsp.	Toasted Cumin
¼ Tsp.	Allspice
1 Tsp.	Tomato Paste
1 Tbsp.	Olive Oil

Method:

- Finely chop the bacon and add to the ground lamb. Combine with the remaining ingredients, and mix well. This can also be done in the food processor if you have one.
- Roll into long meatballs around soaked wooden skewers and grill until desired doneness.
- Serve with couscous and sprinkle with fresh chopped fresh parsley and fresh lemon juice.

Rack of Lamb Stuffed with Brandy Macerated Apricots

Ingredients:

6 to 8	Dried Apricots
1/3 Cup	Brandy or Cognac
1	Rack of Lamb, Frenched (You can have your butcher do this.)
To Taste	Salt and Pepper
1 Tsp.	Thyme
1 Tbsp.	Butter and Olive Oil

Method:

- Finely chop the apricots and place in a bowl. Add the brandy and let the fruit macerate for 1 hour. Meanwhile, allow the lamb to come up to room temperature.
- Pre-heat the oven to 400°.
- Prepare the lamb by cleaning any excess meat or fat from between the bones. The rib bones should be as clean as possible. Reserve any meat scraps for use later in your sauce. Insert a paring knife into the side or the end of the rack of lamb as far in as the knife will go. Turn the rack of lamb and repeat by inserting the paring knife into the other end of the rack of lamb. You are trying to make a cut that goes from one side or end of the rack of lamb to the other. After the cuts have been joined, insert a wooden spoon handle into the slice to make the hole a little larger.
- Drain the brandy from the fruit and set it aside for use later in the sauce. Place a small amount of the finely chopped apricots into the hole that was just created. Using the wooden spoon, press the chopped apricots into the hole half way thru the rack of lamb until tightly packed. Turn over and repeat. Season the rack of lamb with salt, pepper, and thyme.
- Heat a sauté pan for several minutes over high heat. Add the olive oil and the butter. When melted, add the rack of lamb and sauté for 2 minutes on each side or until nicely browned on both sides. Place in oven for 5 to 6 minutes or to desired doneness. Remove from oven, place on a plate, lightly cover with aluminum foil and let rest for several minutes.
- To serve, slice 3 chops per plate, and place on a bed of barley or cheddar cheese mashed potatoes and serve with a Brandy Veal Stock Reduction Sauce. (See in the 'Sauce Recipes' section of the book.)

Variations on a Theme:

Try stuffing the lamb with dried cherries, apples, pears, or peaches.

The Art of Smoking

The technique of smoking foods has been around since man discovered fire. Early man knew, as we do today, that smoking adds an incredible amount of flavor. When smoking meats, it generally takes hours and hours. But if you take the time, I promise it will be well worth the effort. Smoking not only gives flavor to meats, but to vegetables as well. Since vegetables are much more delicate than meat, I generally only smoke them for a couple of hours. Of course the amount of time required depends on the type of vegetable that you are smoking.

There are many type of smokers available, each with its own quirks, plusses, and minuses. I generally use an electric smoker. You should choose one that suits your needs.

With my electric smoker, whether I am smoking chicken, duck, pork, beef, or any other type of meat, the smoker I have is either on or off. It puts out a constant heat of about 200°. If you have a charcoal smoker, charcoal grill, or gas grill, this type of temperature can be obtained by the use of the vents in the charcoal grills. This can also be done by the amount of charcoal that you use. Another thing to consider in charcoal grills is the position of the coals. There are basically 3 ways to position the coals in your grill. One side indirect smoking is where all the coals are located on one side of the grill and the meat is on the other. This method is used for larger cuts of meats such as brisket or a full rack of ribs. The two sided indirect method is used for chickens, game hens or duck. The coals are located on both sides of the grill with the meat in the center. The final method involves evenly scattering the coals on the bottom of the grill. I use this method when I want to sear off vegetables or slices of fruit. For gas grills, using 1 burner in a two-burner grill does this.

There are a couple of ways to turn your charcoal or gas grill into a smoker. For the charcoal grill, you can add water soaked wood chips or chunks right on top of the coals. For gas grills you can pick up a smoker box, add the wood chips in the box and place it directly over the burner being used.

There are a variety of wood types available for smoking foods and they all have their own flavor. The types of wood chips that I find relatively easy to get are mesquite and hickory. These are even available at my grocery store in the summer. If you have a grill store near you, they generally carry a wider variety, such as cherry, pecan, oak, and maple, and you can even get wine or whiskey barrel chips. The barrel chips add a slight sweetness. On the Internet you find an even larger selection. Woods like black walnut, sassafras, peach, mulberry, orange, plum, grape vine…and the list goes on. Do not use pine, fur, or wood from any sappy tree and never use any type of treated wood or lumber.

Smoking Recipes

Smoked Brisket

Ingredients:

6-8 Lb. ....Brisket
2-3 Tbsp...............Street Chef's Beef Brisket Rub (See recipe in the 'Street Chef's Seasoning Mixtures' section of the book.)

Method:
- A whole brisket typically weighs in at 16 to 18 pounds and has three sections: the cap, the point and the flat. The flat is by far the best part and lends itself to even cuts. This is the section that you see most of the time at your grocery store or butcher and it is usually around 6 to 8 pounds. Look for a piece that is well marbled (decent amount of fat evenly distributed throughout the meat). The fat does 2 things, it adds flavor and adds moisture. Trim away any large pieces of fat. This can cause flame flare-ups that can burn the meat.
- To smoke the meat, rub it with the Street Chef's Beef Brisket Rub, place it in the smoker or grill, and smoke with indirect heat until an internal temperature of 190° is reached.

Smoked Chicken

Ingredients:

3 Tsp .... Street Chef's Poultry Seasoning (See recipe in the 'Street Chef's Seasoning Mixtures' section of the book.)
2-3 Tbsp .... Butter, softened
1 Whole .... Chicken

Method:

- Start by mixing a teaspoon of the Street Chef's Poultry Seasonings in 2 to 3 tablespoons of softened butter.
- Rub the butter under the skin and on the outside of the chicken.
- Liberally sprinkle the remaining seasoning mix on the inside and outside of the chicken.
- Place the chicken in a smoker or grill and cook until an internal temperature of 160° is reached. The temperature should be taken between the thigh, the breast and the leg. This will take about 3 to 4 hours, depending on the outside temperature. Let the chicken rest for 5 minutes per pound before carving.
- When using an electric smoker, always finish cooking you chicken in the oven or on a grill to reach an internal temperature of 160°. When in doubt, use a thermometer placed in the thickest part of the chicken, such as the breast.
- Remember to let the chicken rest after it comes out if the oven or off the grill, as it will continue to cook from the residual heat. Letting the chicken rest will allow the juices to redistribute throughout the chicken, making it nice and juicy. Let rest 1 to 2 minutes per pound.
- If you want to just add some smoke flavor, put the chicken in the smoker for about 2 hours and then finish it off in the oven. Or you can add more coals and raise the temperature to around 425° and finish it on the grill. If using a gas grill, just turn on the additional burner and raise the temperature to around 425°. At 425°, a 3½ pound chicken will take about 45 minutes to an hour to cook through.

Smoked Duck Breast

Ingredients:
1 .... Duck Breast

Seasoning Mix
1 Tsp .... Sugar
2 Tsp .... Chili Pasilla, ground
2 Tsp .... Ancho Chile Powder
To Taste .... Salt and Pepper

Sauce
2 Tbsp .... Butter
1 Medium .... Shallot, finely chopped
3 Cups .... Chicken Stock
1 Tsp .... Chipotle Chili Powder
7-8 .... Sage Leaves, finely cut
¼ to ½ Cup .... Heavy Cream
To Taste .... Salt and Pepper

Method:
- Combine the seasoning mix and rub well into both sides of the duck breast. Let marinate at least 1 hour and then place into a smoker and smoke for 2 hours.
- After smoking, place duck breast skin side down in a hot pan and sear until crisp. Then turn the breast over in the pan and place the pan into a 450° oven for 4 to 5 minutes for medium rare.
- For the sauce, place 1 tablespoon of the butter in a sauté pan and sweat the shallot until soft.
- Add the chicken stock and reduce by 2/3.
- Add the chipotle chili powder and 5 or 6 finely cuts sage leaves and cook for 5 minutes.
- Add the cream, bring just to a boil, and reduce until thickened.
- Add salt and pepper to taste, swirl in the last tablespoon of butter and the rest of the finely cut sage leaves.

Smoked Pork Tacos

Ingredients:

1 Tbsp	Cumin
1 Tbsp	Ancho Chili Powder
1 Tsp	Coarse Salt
1 Tsp	Garlic Powder
1 Tsp	Onion Powder
2 Lb	Boneless Pork Roast
20	Corn Tortillas
1 Cup	Peanut Oil
1 Recipe	Pete's Barbecue Sauce or sauce of your choice (See recipe in the 'Sauce' section of the book.)
½ Lb	Cheddar Cheese, grated
1 Head	Lettuce, shredded

Method:

- Mix the first 5 ingredients to make a seasoning mix. Sprinkle the mixture on the pork roast and place in a smoker for 4 to 6 hours.
- Remove the roast from the smoker, and place it in the oven at 350° for 1 hour.
- Remove the roast from the oven and shred the meat.
- Fry the tortillas in hot peanut oil until they just start to get firm. Drape the tortillas over the handle of a wooden spoon to form the taco shells and let them drain and cool.
- When the shells cool, fill with pork, drizzle with barbecue sauce, top with shredded cheese and lettuce, and enjoy!

Smoked Stuffed Tomatoes
(Serves 6)

Ingredients:
½ Lb	Beef Eye Round Steak
1 Link	Andouille Sausage
To Taste	Salt and Pepper
1 Small	Shallot
2-3 Tbsp.	Red Wine
1 Small	Potato
1 Small	Red Pepper
1 Ear	Corn
1 Tsp	Dried Rosemary, crushed by hand
¼ Cup	Goat Cheese
6 Medium	Tomatoes

Method:
- Cut the beef and sausage into ½" cubes and season with salt and pepper. Dice the shallot. Heat a pan over high heat for 2 to 3 minutes. Add the seasoned beef, sausage, and shallots and cook until the beef is browned on both sides.
- Deglaze with a splash of red wine, then remove the pan from the heat and let it cool.
- Dice the potato and red pepper into ½" cubes and cut the kernels from the corn cob. Season with salt, pepper, and rosemary, and cook until golden brown. Remove and add ¼ cup of the goat cheese to the beef and sausage mixture.
- Hollow out the tomatoes by cutting the very top off and scooping out the center (seeds and slime). Then place them in the smoker. After 1 hour, remove the tomatoes from the smoker and place on a serving dish. Spoon the cooled beef mixture into the tomatoes and top with the remainder of the goat cheese.
- Place in 350° oven and cook for 10 to 12 minutes or until golden on top.

Variations on a Theme:
Substitute your favorite sausage or grilled chicken.

Southwestern Smoked Stuffed Tomatoes
(Serves 6)

Ingredients:

¼ Cup	Un-cooked Rice
2 Tsp	Olive Oil
To Taste	Salt and Pepper
¾ Cup	Chicken Stock
2 Links	Chorizo Sausage
1 Small	Shallot, finely chopped
2-3 Tbsp	Red Wine or Spirits
1 Small	Chili Pepper of your choice
1 Tsp.	Mexican Oregano, crushed by hand
½ Tsp	Whole Cumin, toasted and then ground
½ Tsp	Chili Powder (ancho or any other chili powder that you like)
1 Tsp	Paprika
1 Clove	Garlic, finely chopped
6 Medium	Plum Tomatoes

Method:

For the Rice:
- In a medium pot, add a little olive oil and heat over medium heat. Add the un-cooked rice and let cook for 2 to 3 minutes, season with salt and pepper.
- Add ½ cup of the chicken stock, bring to a boil, reduce the heat, and cover and let cook about 15 minutes. Do not remove the cover to check on its progress as this will bring down the temperature inside the pot and it will take longer to cook.
- After 15 minutes turn off the heat and let it rest with the cover on.

For the Stuffing:
- Cut the sausage into ¼" cubes and season with salt and pepper.
- Dice the shallot.
- Heat a pan over high heat for 2 to 3 minutes. Add the sausage and shallots and cook until the sausage is browned.
- Deglaze the pan with a splash of red wine, reduce by half, then remove the pan from the heat and let it cool.
- Dice the chili pepper into ¼" cubes, season with salt, add chili pepper, Mexican oregano, cumin, chili powder, paprika, and garlic and cook until softened and slightly sticking to the pan.
- Deglaze the pan with ¼ cup chicken stock, add the sausage mixture to the pan and combine well. Add the rice to mixture and combine well.

For the Tomatoes:
- Hollow out the tomatoes by cutting the very top off and scooping out the center – the seeds and slime. Then place the tomatoes in the smoker for 1 hour.
- Remove the tomatoes from the smoker and place on a serving dish. Spoon the cooled sausage and rice mixture into the tomatoes. (For a finishing touch, you can add a little grated cheese to the tops).
- Place the filled tomatoes into a 350° oven and cook for 10 to 12 minutes or until golden on top.

Tea-Smoked Duck

Ingredients:
1 .... Duck Breast
1 to 2 Tbsp .... Chinese 5 Spice
.... Black Tea
To Taste .... Salt and White Pepper

Method:
- Season the duck breast with Chinese 5 Spice and marinate 1 hour.
- After marinating, place the duck breast into smoker with black tea instead of wood chips and smoke for 2 hours, replacing the tea in the smoker as needed.
- After smoking, sprinkle the duck breast with salt and white pepper and sear over high heat, skin side down. After turning onto the second side, finish in a 350° oven to desired doneness.

How to Cut Up a Chicken

Learning how to cut up a chicken is a great way to save money and buying whole chickens and cutting them up yourself means you have the leftover carcass for use in making stock. Saving the cavity, wing tips, and leftover bones from making wing drumettes or boneless thighs will add to the richness of your stock. With a little practice, a whole chicken can be cut up in a several minutes. To begin, make sure your knife is sharp. Then, rinse the chicken inside and out and pat it dry.

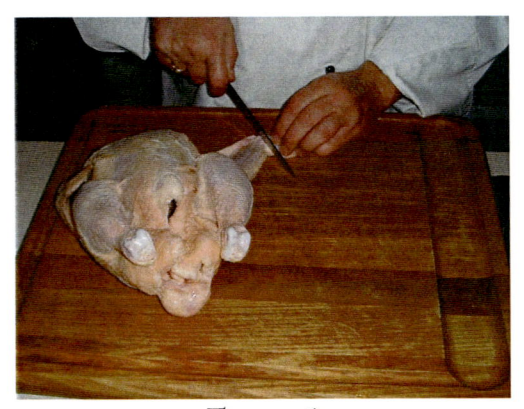

Figure 1

Start by cutting the first wing tip off. Feel for where the joint moves. Between each joint there is a small area that your knife will cut through with very little resistance. Extend the joint and cut through that joint. If cutting through is difficult, try moving the knife from one side or the other. The knife should cut through the joint very easily.

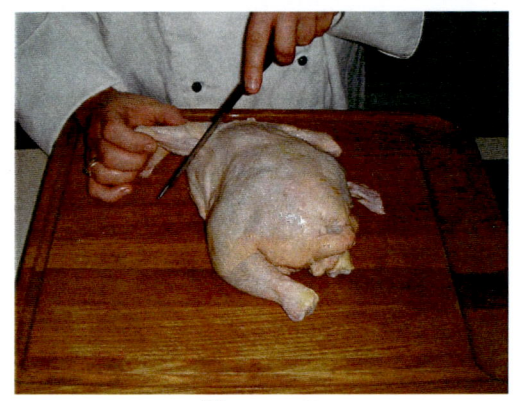

Figure 2

Next, move to the wing joint that connects the wing to the body. Make a small cut though the skin. See how the wing attaches to the body. Generally there is a small line of fat at each joint; this is your guide to follow with your knife. Make a slice. Look at the joint while pulling the wing back and slice through the joint. Your knife should go through easily.

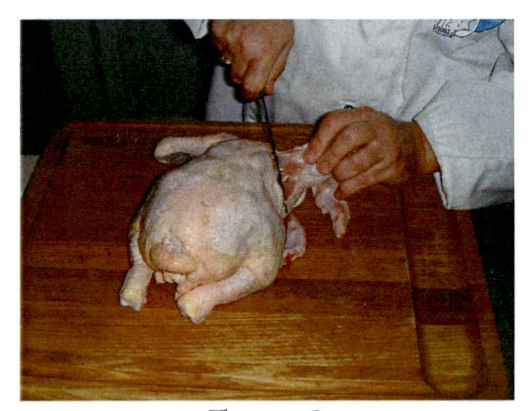

Figure 3

This photo shows the knife going through the wing joint.

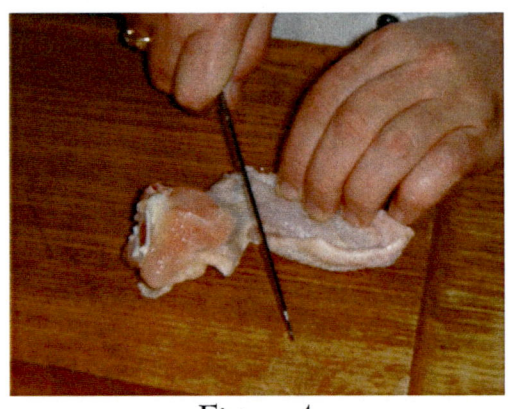

Figure 4

Now cut the middle joint. There is a small ridge you can find with your finger. Your knife should go through the joint very easily.

104 • How to Cut Up a Chicken

Figure 5

Pull the leg away from the chicken body and make a slice through the skin.

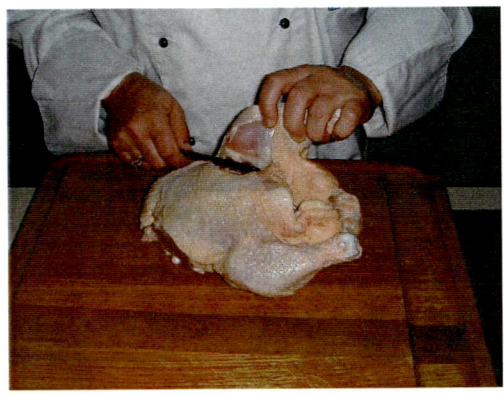

Figure 6

As you pull the leg from the body, you will notice where the leg and the thigh meet. There is a line of fat separating them. This line will guide you as you begin your cut.

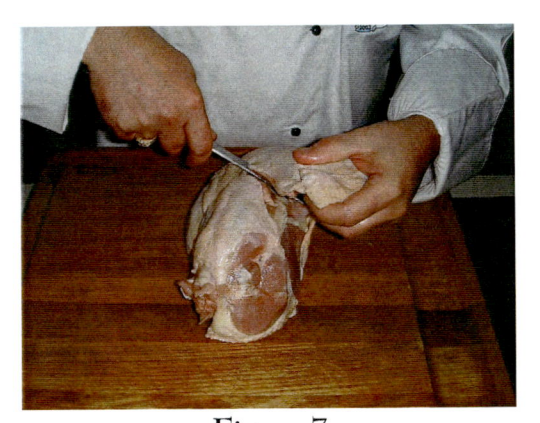

Figure 7

Continue cutting through the line of fat and around the body to the back of the chicken. Where the thigh attaches to the body at the back, there is a small half circle, called the oyster. Many claim this small section of the thigh is the most tender and flavorful part of the chicken.

The Street Chef • 105

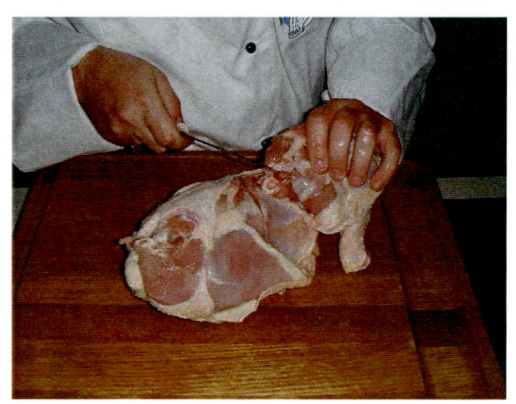

Figure 8

Pull the chicken thigh back to expose the joint. Pull back the thigh to break the joint. Now finish cutting the thigh off, following the body contour.

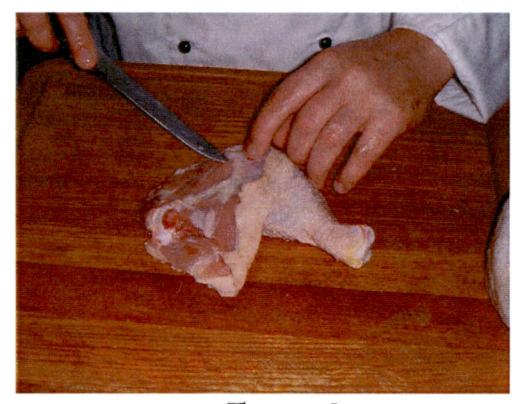

Figure 9

Notice the line of fat showed between the knife blade and the finger. This is where you make your next cut. Feel for the ridge between the thigh and the leg. When your knife cuts through this section, it should cut through very easily.

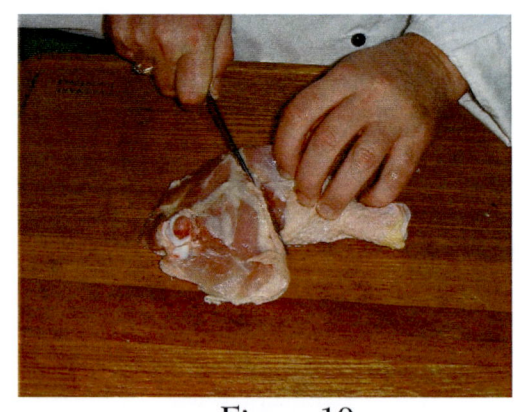

Figure 10

Slice all the way through the meat between the leg and the thigh.

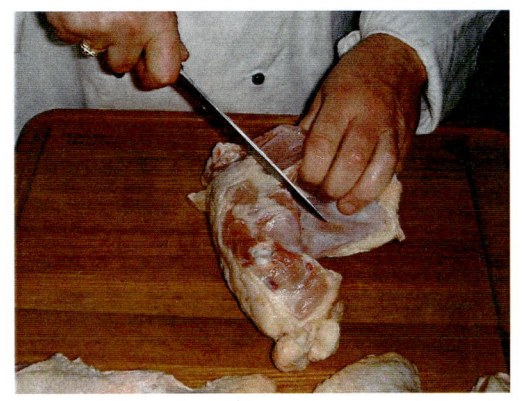

Figure 11

Slice through the ribs on both sides to remove the breast section from the body.

Figure 12

Place the knife between the breasts, and carefully slice through the breast sections. Turn and slice the rear section of the breast. See below.

Figure 13

Figure 14

Here is a photograph showing what your cut up chicken should look like.

Lollipop Chicken Wings

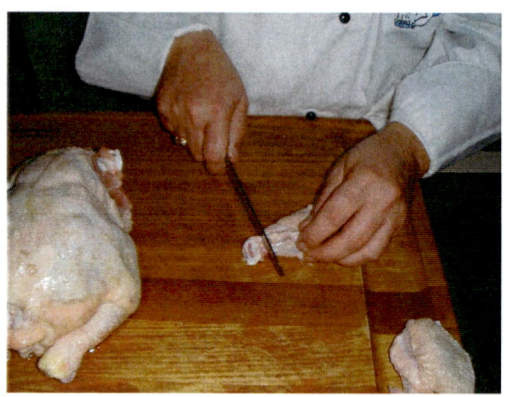

Figure 15

To make Chicken Wing Lollipops, start with the larger section of the wing.

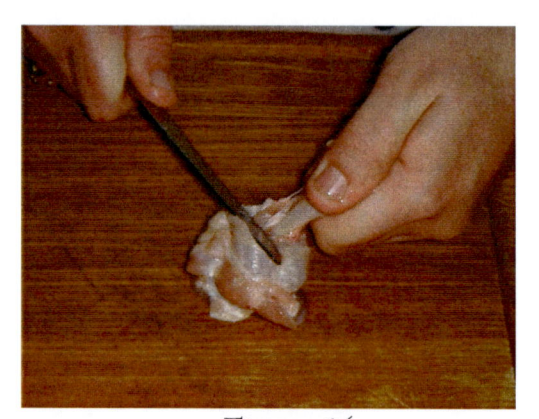

Figure 16

Holding the top of the wing, scrape the meat from the top of the wing, down the joint below. Keep turning the wing around until all the meat is at the bottom of the wing joint.

108 • How to Cut Up a Chicken

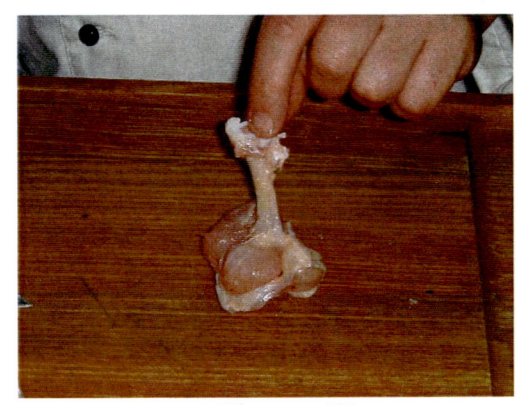

Figure 17

Clean the top of the joint and this is what the wing should look like when finished.

Chicken and Other Poultry Recipes

Brine

Brining is an age-old process of soaking meat in a saltwater/seasoned water bath. It is used mostly for preserving meats and making them moister, but some flavor can also be added. Currently the most popular uses are for turkeys at Thanksgiving and for chicken, but brining works for other meats and seafood as well.

While in the brine, the meat cells absorb liquid which keeps the meat moist. Try brining your skinless, boneless chicken breasts and see how much moister they are. One of the biggest problems with chicken breasts is that they dry out and turn to rubber (or worse). Brining will eliminate that problem. Pork chops are great for brining as well.

A good, basic recipe is ½ cup of kosher salt and ½ cup of sugar to 1 gallon of water. If you want to spice things up a bit, you can use a different liquid. You can use apple juice, apple cider, apple cider vinegar, rice wine vinegar, orange juice, stock, tea, beer, wine, or other liquids to replace some or all of the water. You can also put spices in as flavor enhances. Some popular choices are garlic, onion, thyme, oregano, (really any dried herb of your choice), citrus zest, and pickling spice.

The amount of brining time depends on the thickness of the meat and the strength of the brine. See the table below for some suggested times. If you are brining meat for more than an hour, it must be kept refrigerated. And make sure it is fully submerged. Weigh it down with a heavy plate if necessary.

Here are a few suggestions for different meats:

Meat	Brine Ingredients	Time
Large Whole Chicken	½ cup of salt and ½ cup of sugar to 2 quarts of water	3 to 4 hours
Chicken Pieces	¼ cup of salt and ¼ cup of sugar to 1 quart of water	2 hours
Cornish Hens	¼ cup of salt and ¼ cup of sugar to 2 quarts of water	1 hour
Pork Chops	¼ cup of salt and ¼ cup of sugar to 1 quart of water	4 hours
Turkey Breast	¼ cup of salt and ¼ cup of sugar to 1 quart of water	4 to 6 hours
Turkey	1 cup of salt and 1 cup of sugar to 1 gallon of water	12 to 24 hours

Many people start the brine with hot water to more easily dissolve the salt and sugar. If you do this, remember the solution must be cooled completely before you add the meat. Never put raw meat into warm or hot water to brine.

Citrus Marinated Chicken

Ingredients:

2	Oranges, juiced
1	Lime, juiced
Zest of 1	Orange
Zest of 1	Lime
1	Grapefruit, juiced
1	Lemon, juiced
1½ Tsp	Brown Sugar
2 Tbsp	Dark Rum
½	Dried New Mexico Chile, or Chile of your choice, chopped
1	Serrano Chile, seeded and chopped
6	Chicken Breasts or Thighs
To Taste	Salt and Pepper
4 Tbsp	Butter (optional)
½	White Onion, finely chopped and caramelized

Method:

- Zest the orange and lime. Juice all the citrus.
- Combine the zest, juice, and remaining ingredients except for the salt and pepper and caramelized onions, to form a marinade.
- Marinate the chicken for at least 2-3 hours up to overnight if possible.
- Remove the chicken from the marinade, season with salt and pepper, and grill over medium heat until done.
- Strain the remaining marinade to remove any solids and reduce over medium heat to form a sauce. For richer sauce, before serving, remove from the heat and add 4 tablespoons of butter cut into cubes, stirring to incorporate.
- Serve the chicken over caramelized onions and drizzle with sauce.

General Tso's Chicken

<u>Ingredients:</u>

Sauce

½ Cup	Cornstarch
¼ Cup	Water
2 Tsp	Garlic, minced
2 Tbsp	Gingerroot, minced
½ Cup	Sugar
½ Cup	Soy Sauce
¼ Cup	White Vinegar
¼ Cup	Rice Wine or Sherry
1 ½ Cups	Chicken Stock
1 Tsp	MSG (optional)

Meat

¼ Cup	Soy Sauce
1 Tsp	White Pepper
1	Egg
1 Cup	Cornstarch
3 Lbs	Dark Chicken Meat, de-boned and cut into large chunks
	Vegetable oil for deep-frying

Stir-Fry

1-2 Tbsp	Oil
2 Cups	Green Onions, sliced
16 Small	Dried Hot Peppers

<u>Method:</u>

For the Sauce:
- Mix ½ cup cornstarch with ¼ cup of water.
- Add garlic, ginger, sugar, soy sauce, vinegar, wine, chicken stock and MSG (if desired) and stir until sugar dissolves. Refrigerate until needed.

For the Chicken:
- In a separate bowl, mix soy sauce and white pepper. Stir in egg. Add cornstarch and mix to combine.
- Add the chicken pieces and get them coated evenly. Divide chicken into small quantities and deep-fry at 350° until crispy. Drain on paper towels.

For the Stir-Fry:
- Place a small amount of oil in wok and heat until wok is hot. Add onions and peppers and stir-fry briefly. Stir the sauce and add to wok. Place chicken in sauce and cook until sauce thickens.

Pan-Seared Chicken and Wild Mushrooms

Ingredients:

6	Chicken Breasts or Thighs (I prefer thighs), cut into 1" pieces
2 Tbsp	Street Chef Poultry Seasoning or Poultry Seasoning of your choice (See recipe in 'Street Chef's Seasoning Mixtures' section of the book.)
2 Tbsp	Olive Oil
¼ to ½ Lb	Chanterelle Mushrooms, roughly chopped (You can also use a mixture of different types of mushrooms)
1 Small	Shallot, finely chopped
2 Cloves	Garlic, finely chopped
½ Cup	White Wine
½ Cup	Chicken Stock
1 Tsp	Fresh Thyme
1 Tsp	Dried Tarragon
¼ Cup	Cream (optional)
1 Tbsp	Butter (optional)
To Taste	Salt and Pepper

Method:

- Season the chicken with the poultry seasoning. Heat a medium sauté pan over medium-high heat. Add some olive oil to the pan, add the chicken in small batches and sear well. Remove from the pan and drain.
- When done with the chicken, cook the mushrooms in the same pan over medium-high heat. Again, you want to sear the mushrooms in small batches. Remove when finished cooking and reserve.
- In the same pan, lower the heat to medium and add the shallots and garlic. Deglaze with the wine, and reduce by half.
- Add the chicken stock and raise the heat to medium-high. Add the thyme and the tarragon and cook for 2 to 3 minutes.
- Add the chicken and mushrooms and cook about 3 to 4 minutes to finish cooking the chicken.
- Add the cream if desired and cook for 1 to 2 minutes.
- Turn the heat off and swirl in the butter. Serve over rice.

Pan-Seared Duck Breast with Blackberry Veal Stock Reduction

Ingredients:

1 Pkg. .... Mascovy Duck Breasts (2 halves, about 8 ounces each)
To Taste .... Salt and Pepper

Method:

- Pre-heat the oven to 350°. Heat a sauté pan over medium-high heat for several minutes before adding the duck breast.
- Season both sides of the duck breast with salt and pepper. Place in the sauté pan, skin side down, and cook for 3 to 4 minutes or until golden brown. Turn the duck breast over and cook 2 more minutes, then place it in the oven to finish cooking. I usually give it about 8 minutes, as I like the duck served medium rare.
- Reserve the duck fat. Strain it through a fine mesh strainer and let cool. Place in a container and freeze. Duck fat is wonderful to use for fried potatoes or potato cakes.
- Slice the duck breasts and serve with the Rice Pilaf with Dried Cranberries and Toasted Pine Nuts. (See recipe in the 'A Little Something on the Side' section of the book.)

Roast Duck Asian Style

(Serves 3 to 4)

Ingredients:

Sauce

1/3 Cup	Sake
2/3 Cup	Soy Sauce
4 Tbsp	Fresh Ginger, finely chopped
¼ Cup	Balsamic Vinegar
1 Tbsp	Sugar
1 Tbsp	Chinese Barbecue Sauce
2 Tbsp	Ginger, minced
¼ Tsp	Ground White Pepper

Duck

1 - 4 to 5 Lb.	Mascovy or Long Island Duck. For this recipe I use Mascovy as they have a larger breast than Long Island ducks.
1	Lime, quartered
3" Piece	Ginger, peeled and roughly chopped.
3 Tbsp	Hoisin Sauce
1 Recipe	Basic Crepes
½ Cup	Spring Onions, sliced

Method:

- In a 2-quart pan, mix together the ingredients for the sauce, place over medium-low heat and reduce by half. Set aside ¼ cup of the sauce. Wash and pat the duck dry. Glaze the inside and outside of the duck with some of the non-reserved sauce.
- Pre-heat the oven to 450°.
- Place the lime and ginger inside the cavity of the duck. Place the duck on a rack in a roasting pan, breast side down, and place in the oven. Bake 20 minutes, lower the oven temperature to 350°, rotate the duck to be breast-side-up, and glaze with more of the sauce mixture. Cook 40 minutes. Check for doneness. I like to serve my roast duck a little pink, so I remove it from the oven at about 130° to 135°. Remember to let the duck rest after removing it from the oven. It will continue to cook and rise another 5 to 8 degrees from the residual heat. If you like it cooked well done, cook until desired doneness.

- While the duck is resting, mix together in a small bowl the reserved ¼ cup sauce and the 3 tablespoons of Hoisin sauce.
- Slice the skin off the duck and reserve. Slice the meat into small slices.
- Serve in crepes. (See Basic Crepe recipe in the 'Pastry and Dessert Recipes' section of the book.)
- Lay the crepes flat, smear a tablespoon of the sauce mixture on the crepe, place several slices of duck, and some of the duck skin, followed by sliced spring onions and roll into a wrap.
- Serve with fried rice and a mixed green salad.

Szechwan Chicken
(Serves 3 to 4)

Ingredients:
3-4	Chicken Breasts, skinned and boned
2	Egg Whites
2 Tbsp	Cornstarch

Sauce
2 Tbsp	Sherry
1 Tbsp	Hoisin Sauce
2 Tbsp	Sesame Oil
1 Tbsp	Soy Sauce
2 Tbsp	Brown Sugar
¼ Tsp	Cayenne Pepper
½ to 1 Tsp	Dried Chilies, crushed
2 Tbsp	Ginger, minced
4	Carrots, cut into thin strips
3	Green Onions, cut on the diagonal
½	Red Pepper, sliced
½	Yellow Pepper, sliced

Method:
- Partially freeze chicken breasts. Cut into strips.
- Combine sauce ingredients and set aside.
- Mix together egg whites and cornstarch. Coat chicken in cornstarch mixture.
- Heat wok. Fry chicken strips in oil until they turn white. Place on paper towels to drain, and reserve.
- Add 1 tablespoon oil to wok, add vegetables, and stir-fry for 30 seconds.
- Add sauce to vegetables and bring to a boil. When boiling, add chicken and stir-fry 1 to 2 minutes. Serve with rice.

Tequila Chicken

Ingredients:

1 Tbsp	Olive Oil
1 Tbsp	Butter
1 Medium	Onion, diced
1 Large Clove	Garlic, minced
Chicken Thighs	Cut into ¾" pieces, marinated in ¼ Cup of Tequila and Juice of ½ a Lime
4 Links	Chorizo Sausage, parboiled until they hold together
¼ Cup	Tequila
Juice of ½	Lime
3 Cups	Chicken Stock
20	Saffron Threads
2 Tbsp	Tomato Paste
¼ Cup	Cream
To Taste	Salt and Pepper

Seasoning Mix

1 Tsp.	Ancho Chili Powder
¼ Tsp	Cinnamon
½ Tsp	Cumin
¼ Tsp	Oregano
¼ Tsp	Onion Powder/Garlic
½ Tsp	Hot Paprika

Method:

- Pre-heat a medium saucepan for 5 minutes, then add the olive oil, butter and onions and cook until soft, but not browned. Add the garlic and cook for 2 minutes.
- Mix together the ingredients for the seasoning mix.
- Add ¼ teaspoon of the seasoning mix to the onions in the pan and cook until the mixture starts to stick to the pan. Remove the onions and set aside.
- Remove the chicken from the marinade, but reserve the marinade for later use. (When using reserved marinade, always make sure it is brought to a boil to eliminate any bacteria.)
- Add the chicken, seasoned with 1 teaspoon of the seasoning mix, to the pan and cook until the chicken is golden brown.
- Add the Chorizo and sprinkle with seasoning mix. Deglaze with the reserved chicken marinade. Cook until most of the moisture has evaporated.
- Deglaze again with an additional ¼ cup of tequila and the remaining limejuice. Cook until almost dry. Add the chicken stock, the remaining seasoning mix, the saffron and the tomato paste. Cook until it reduces by ½. Add the cream right before serving and heat for 5 minutes. Add salt and pepper is necessary.
- Serve over Homemade Pasta or pasta of your choice.

Seafood

Many people are hesitant when it comes to cooking seafood and think it's too difficult. But it's really not so bad. There are many things you can do with fish. It can be fried, baked, smoked, and even grilled.

The first and most important thing I can recommend is that you get to know your fish monger. Whether you purchase your seafood from your local grocery store, from a specialty store, or from a seafood shop, talk to the people who work there. They are the people with the best information on which fish is right for your specific need and which fish is the freshest on any given day.

You also need to inspect the fish. If the fish monger won't let you inspect or smell the fish, look for another place to purchase your fish. Why do you need to smell it? Because looks can be deceiving, especially with fish that is already cleaned and cut up. You might see a nice Mako shark steak and it could look just fine. But don't buy it until you smell it. If it smells like ammonia, don't buy it. When looking at whole fish, look for bright red gills, clear eyes, and the smell of the sea. If the fish is slimy or smells like a pier, it is not fresh.

When it comes to seafood, be flexible. Don't give up if you can't find the exact fish called for in a recipe. If a recipe calls for rockfish, but rockfish isn't in season, make the recipe with another type of fish. You'll be surprised how good it is. Flounder, trout, white bass, and orange roughy are all interchangeable.

There are several categories of fish. Flounder, fluke, Dover sole, halibut, and turbot, are just of few of the many types of flat fish. When flat fish are born, they have eyes on both their sides of their head. As they mature, one eye migrates to the opposite side. Adult flatfish do not have spines.

Bass, salmon, trout, cod, pike, and tuna are all round fish. Round fish have a spine near the top of their body and have one eye on each side of their head regardless of the age of the fish.

Skate, rays, sharks and monkfish are cartilaginous fish. Monkfish are sometimes called the poor man's lobster because their texture and taste are so similar to lobster. Skate is not real easy to find, partly because it goes bad so quickly and, when it goes bad it smells awful! Make sure you use skate the same day you buy it. In fact, it's not a bad rule of thumb with most seafood to use it within 24 to 36 hours of purchasing it.

Seafood Recipes

Bill's Shrimp and Feta over Spaghetti Squash

Ingredients:

1 Small	Spaghetti Squash
1 Tbsp	Olive Oil
1 Medium	Shallot, finely chopped
½ Lb.	Medium Shrimp, peeled and de-veined
¼ Cup	White Wine
1 Medium	Tomato, cut into small dice
2 oz.	Feta Cheese (Herb and Garlic flavored or your favorite cheese)
½ - 2/3 Cup	Cream
To Taste	Salt and Freshly Ground Pepper

Method:

- Pre-heat oven to 400°. Cut spaghetti squash in half and remove the seeds. Place on a baking sheet cut side down for 1 hour.
- While the squash is baking, pre-heat a sauté pan over medium-high heat. Add olive oil and shallots and let cook until soft.
- Add the shrimp and cook 2 minutes on each side. Remove and set aside.
- Deglaze the pan with the white wine and add the diced tomato, crumbled feta cheese and cream. Cook until thickened (about 5 to 10 minutes).
- Lower the heat to a simmer and add the shrimp to finish cooking and to absorb the flavors. Add salt and pepper to taste.
- Remove the spaghetti squash from the oven and scrape out the insides. The squash will look just like spaghetti.
- Place the desired amount on a plate and spoon the shrimp and sauce on top. Garnish with fresh basil and thyme and serve.

Crawfish Egg Rolls

Ingredients:

1 Lb.	Crawfish Tails
2 Tbsp	Cajun Seasoning Mix (See recipe in the 'Street Chef's Seasoning Mixtures' section of the book.)
1 Tbsp.	Butter
1 Tbsp	Olive Oil
¼ Cup	Red Bell Pepper, cut into a small dice
1/8 Cup	Celery, cut into a small dice
½ Cup	Onions, cut into a small dice
1 Tsp	Dried Basil
1 Tsp	Dried Thyme
1 Tsp	Dried Oregano
¼ Cup	Brandy
1 ¼ Cup	Heavy Cream
2 Tbsp.	Tomato Paste
1 Pkg.	Lumpia Wrappers (available at your Asian grocer)

Method:

- Wash the crawfish tails and pat dry. Sprinkle 1 tablespoon of the seasoning on the crawfish.
- Heat a 4-quart sauté pan over medium-high heat for several minutes, then add the butter and olive oil. Add the crawfish, cook for 2 minutes to sear the spice mixture to the crawfish, remove from the heat and reserve.
- Add the bell pepper, celery and the onions and cook 3 to 4 minutes until softened. Add the remaining Cajun seasoning mix and the dried herbs, cook until the vegetables start to stick to the pan. Add the brandy to deglaze the pan. Cook until reduced by half. Add the cream and the tomato paste. Cook until thickened.
- Stir in the crawfish, cook 1 minute. Remove from the heat and let cool.
- To make the egg rolls, spoon about 2 to 3 tablespoons of the filling onto the upper third of each wrapper in the corner. Fold the corner over the filling to the mid point and lightly press down. Fold the right corner toward the middle, then fold the left corner toward the middle. At this point it should like a round open letter. Now roll the round section to the last corner and seal the egg roll with a little water.

Variations on a Theme:

Add 1 cup of chicken stock to the sauce and serve over pasta of your choice. Top with freshly grated parmesan cheese.

Crawfish Etouffee
(Serves 8)

Ingredients:

¾ Cup	Oil
¾ Cup	Flour
2 Tbsp	Seafood Creole Seasoning, or more if you like it hot (See recipe in the 'Street Chef's Seasoning Mixtures' section of the book.)
¼ Cup	Onion, finely chopped
¼ Cup	Celery, peeled and finely chopped
¼ Cup	Bell Pepper, I like red, yellow, or orange the best
3 Cups	Seafood Stock (at room temp)
1½ Sticks	Butter
2 Lbs	Crawfish Tails
½ Cup	Green Onions
½ Cup	Fresh Parsley, finely chopped
1 Tbsp	Fresh Garlic Paste
¼ Cup	White Wine
2 Tsp	Tabasco Pepper Sauce

Method:

- Heat oil over medium-high heat (let pan heat for several minutes before adding the flour) and whisk in the flour. Cook the roux, stirring constantly, until it turns a dark brown color.
- Add 1 tablespoon of Seafood Creole Seasoning, onions, celery and bell peppers. Cook until the vegetables are tender. Don't let the mixture burn or you will have to start over again. Remember stir, stir, and stir. The roux should be done in about 20 minutes.
- Slowly add 2 cups of the cooled seafood stock to the hot roux, stirring constantly until completely dissolved. Remove from the heat and cover.
- Heat half of the butter in a sauté pan over medium-high heat. While the butter is melting, add half of the remaining seasoning mix to the crawfish tails. Sear the tails in the butter until the seasoning has a bronze color to it.
- Add the green onions, parsley and garlic paste, stir and deglaze with white wine. Cook until the wine has almost evaporated, then add the Tabasco sauce.
- Slowly add the remaining stock and start shaking the pan back and forth. Add the remaining butter a little at a time. If the sauce starts to break, add a little water or butter.
- Serve immediately over rice.

Grilled Fish Tacos
(Serves 12)

Ingredients:

2 Tbsp	Ground Cumin
2 Tbsp	Ancho Chili Powder
1 Tsp	Dried Oregano, powdered in your hand
2 Tsp.	Salt
1 Tsp.	Black Pepper
2 to 3 Tbsp	Tequila
Juice of 2	Limes
Zest of 1	Lime
Pinch	Sugar
½ Large	White Onion, finely sliced
2 Cloves	Garlic, minced
3 Tbsp + 1 Cup	Olive Oil
½ Cup + 1 Cup	Cilantro, ½ Cup finely chopped, 1 Cup Leaves
2 lbs	Mahi Mahi, or any other firm white fish
24	Tortillas
2 to 3	Tomatoes, peeled, seeded and cut into ½" dice
2 Cups	Lettuce, shredded

Method:

- While preparing the ingredients below, start the grill. If you are going to smoke the fish, soak the chips in water if you are using a gas grill or charcoal smoker.
- In a small bowl, combine the cumin, ancho, oregano, salt, and pepper. This is your seasoning mix.
- In a large bowl, mix the tequila, lime juice, lime zest, sugar, white onions, garlic, 3 tablespoons olive oil, ¼ cup of finely chopped cilantro and half the seasoning mix. Stir to combine, pour over fish and let marinate for at least ½ hour. An hour would be better. Any longer and the tequila and lime juice will start to cook the fish.
- After the fish has marinated, remove and scrape off the excess oil. Sprinkle the remaining seasoning mix on both sides and pat into the fish.
- Prepare cilantro oil by placing 1 cup of olive oil into a blender. Add 1 cup of cilantro leaves. Blend for one minute. Pour the mixture thru a fine mesh strainer into a bowl or a squeeze bottle.
- Place the fish over hot coals and cook 1 to 2 minutes per side or until done. The amount of time will depend on the thickness of the fish. When the fish is done, flake the fish in a bowl and add the remaining ¼ cup finely chopped cilantro.
- To build your tacos, fill tortillas with fish, tomatoes, lettuce, cilantro oil and your favorite salsa.

Herb Crusted Rock Fish with Sauce Beurre Blanc

Ingredients:

6 to 8 Tbsp	Fresh Herbs (thyme, tarragon, and parsley)
1 Tbsp	Olive Oil
2	Rockfish Fillets or 6 Steaks
To Taste	Salt and Pepper
½ to 1 Stick	Butter, cut into ½" blocks
1 Small	Shallot, finely chopped
½ Cup	White Wine or Champagne

You can use any nice white fish for this - trout, flounder, grouper, rockfish, etc.

To save time and trouble, have your fishmonger fillet the fish for you.

Method:
- Finely chop the herbs. You can use one or all of the herbs listed above.
- Pour a little olive oil on the fish fillet and roll the fish in the fresh herbs. Then salt and pepper them on both sides.
- Heat a pan over medium to high heat for several minutes.
- Pour a little olive oil and a small amount of butter in the pan and add the fillets, presentation side down and sear both sides until golden. Remove from the heat and set aside. The fish should be slightly under-cooked at this point.
- In the same pan (drain used oil and butter) add a small pat of butter and let it melt. Then add the shallots and ½ cup of white wine. Let the mixture simmer until almost dry and turn the heat down to low. Slowly add cold butter chunks over very low temperature whisking constantly. The more butter you add, the thicker the sauce will become. You can also add your favorite herbs; tarragon, thyme and dill would work nicely. If you want to add herbs to the recipe, add half the amount you plan to use with the shallots and save the remainder to sprinkle over the finished dish.

Variations on a Theme:
- Use lemon, lime, orange, or grapefruit juice instead of the wine. I like lime and cilantro oil drizzled on top.
- Place the fish fillets on a plate and drizzle the sauce over the fillets. Serve with baby carrots and roasted potatoes or sautéed julienne of carrot, squash and zucchini.

Tip: If you'd like to serve wine with this dish, a Sauvignon Blanc or Pinot Grigio would go nicely.

Pan-Seared Salmon Steaks with Sauce Beurre Blanc

Ingredients:
Salmon
4 .... Salmon Steaks
1 Tbsp .... Butter
1 Tbsp .... Olive Oil
To Taste .... Salt and Fresh Ground Pepper
Pinch or so .... Sugar

Salmon Marinade (if you want to marinate)
1 Cup.................... White Wine
Zest of 1 Each ...... Lemon and Lime

Sauce Beurre-Blanc
½ to ¾ Cup .... White Wine
2 Tbsp .... Shallots
1 Stick .... Butter, cut into ¼" cubes (butter should be cold)
¼ cup................... Heavy cream (optional)

Method:
- Prepare the marinade and marinate the steaks for 1 hour.
- Heat a sauté pan over medium-high heat for about 5 minutes.
- Place 1 tablespoon butter in the hot pan and heat until slightly brown. Then add the olive oil.
- Sprinkle salt, pepper, and sugar on both sides of the fish and place the salmon in the sauté pan. Let cook for 3 minutes or until the outside of the steaks has caramelized. Check by sliding a spatula under the fish and peeking. When the steak has caramelized, flip the steak and cook the other side until caramelized. Remove the steaks from the pan and keep them warm in a 300° oven while making the sauce.
- Pour the butter and oil used to cook the salmon steaks out of the pan and re-heat it over medium-high heat.
- Deglaze with the white wine, stirring up any bits let over from the steaks. Add the shallots and cook until almost dry. Remove the pan from the heat and start slowly adding the butter, stirring constantly to form an emulsion. Add cream if desired.
- When the sauce is done, remove the salmon steaks from the oven, place on a plate and spoon the sauce over the steaks to serve.

Pan-Seared White Fish

Ingredients:
4	Fish Fillets
To Taste	Salt and Pepper
1 Tbsp	Olive Oil
½ Stick	Butter, cut into ½" cubes
1 Small	Shallot, finely chopped
½ Cup	White Wine
2 Tbsp	Vinegar
2 Tbsp	Fresh Herbs

You can use any nice white fish for this - trout, flounder, grouper, rockfish, etc.
To save time and trouble, have your fishmonger fillet the fish for you.

Method:
- Salt and pepper the fish fillets on both sides while heating a pan over medium to high heat for several minutes.
- Pour a little olive oil and a small amount of butter in the pan and add the fillets, presentation side down. Sear both sides until golden, remove from heat, and set aside. The fish should be slightly under-cooked at this point.
- Drain the used oil and butter from the pan, add a small pat of butter, and let it melt. Add shallots, HALF the herbs, ½ cup of white wine, and a good splash of vinegar. You can use apple cider, rice wine or your favorite vinegar.
- Let the mixture simmer until almost dry and slowly add cold butter chunks over very low temperature whisking constantly. The more butter you add, the thicker the sauce will become.
- Place the fish fillets on a plate, drizzle the sauce over the fillets, and sprinkle with the remaining herbs. Serve with baby carrots and roasted potatoes or sautéed julienne of carrot, squash and zucchini.

Variations on a Theme:
Use lemon, lime, and orange or grapefruit juice instead of the vinegar. I like lime and cilantro oil drizzled on top.

Tip: Sauvignon Blanc or Pinot Grigio wines will complement this nicely.

Poached Salmon with Citrus Butter Sauce

Ingredients:
4 .... Fresh Salmon Steaks

Poaching Liquid
Equal Parts .... White Wine and Water
.... Remaining Marinade
1 to 2 Tsp .... Salt
To Taste .... Fresh Ground Pepper

Salmon Marinade
.... White wine
Zest of 1 Each ...... Lemon and Lime

Citrus Butter Sauce
2 Tbsp .... Shallots, finely chopped
Juice of 2 Each ..... Lemons and Limes
To Taste .... Salt and Pepper
1 Tsp .... Sugar
1 Stick .... Butter, cut into ¼" cubes (butter should be cold)

Method:
- Prepare the poaching liquid and place in a pan that is deep enough for the marinade and the salmon steaks.
- Marinate the salmon steaks for 1 hour.
- Drain the marinade into the poaching liquid and bring to a slow boil. Reduce heat to a mere simmer. Slowly add the salmon steaks and poach the salmon for 8 to 10 minutes or until it reaches the desired doneness.
- While the salmon is poaching, heat a sauté pan over medium-high heat. Add shallots, lemon-lime juice, salt, pepper, and sugar and cook until almost dry. Remove the pan from the heat and start slowly adding the butter, stirring constantly to form an emulsion.
- When the salmon steaks are done, remove them from the poaching liquid and remove the skin and bones.
- Place the salmon steaks on a plate and spoon the sauce over them to serve.

Seven Spice Shrimp and Mango Salsa

Ingredients:
1	Star Anise
1 Tsp.	Coriander
¼ Tsp.	Nutmeg
¼ Tsp.	Allspice
¼ Tsp.	Cardamom
¼ Tsp.	Powdered Ginger
½ Lb.	Shrimp, peeled and de-veined
	Cornstarch
	Peanut Oil
1 Dried	Cayenne Pepper
	Mango Salsa (See recipe in the 'Sauce Recipes' section of this book)

Method:
- Grind first six spices together. Sprinkle over both sides of the shrimp, and then lightly coat the shrimp in cornstarch.
- Heat peanut oil in a sauté pan along with the dried pepper. Add the shrimp and cook through.
- Serve with Mango Salsa.

Shrimp Creole
(Serves 10)

Ingredients:

3½ Lbs.	Shrimp, with the shells on. If you can find shrimp with the heads on, buy them.
3 Tbsp	Seafood Creole Seasoning, or more if you like it hot (See recipe in 'Street Chef's Seasoning Mixtures' section of the book.)
14	Ripe Plum Tomatoes
3 Cups	Onion, finely chopped
2 Sprigs	Fresh Thyme
2	Bay Leaves
5	Peppercorns
3 Sprigs	Fresh Parsley
1½ Cups	White Wine
¼ Cup	Butter
1¼ Cups	Celery, peeled and finely chopped
1½ Cups	Bell Pepper (I like red, yellow, or orange the best)
1 Tbsp	Fresh Garlic Paste
2 Tsp	Tabasco Pepper Sauce
1½ Cups	Tomato Sauce
2 to 3 Tsp	Cane Syrup or Sugar

Method:

- Clean, peel and rinse the shrimp using cold water. Reserve the shrimp shells for the stock. Season the shrimp with 1 tablespoon of the seafood seasoning and place in the refrigerator until needed.
- You need to roast the tomatoes. Start by slicing the tomatoes in half and removing the seeds. Place them cut side down on a sheet tray and bake at 350° until blackened on top. Let them cool. Then remove and discard the skins. Set the tomatoes aside.
- For the seafood stock, add all of the shrimp shells into a pot large enough to hold the shells. Add ½ cup of chopped onions, thyme, bay leaf, peppercorns and the parsley. Add ½ cup white wine and 2½ cups of cold water to the pot. Bring the ingredients to a boil and skim the top to remove any impurities. Lower the heat to a simmer and cook 20 minutes. Strain the stock and discard the shrimp shells and return stock to the pot to reduce to 1½ cups. Reserve.
- Heat ¼ cup of butter over high heat until melted and add 1½ cups of the onion stirring constantly for 4 minutes. Reduce the heat to medium-high and continue cooking until caramelized.
- Add 1 teaspoon of seafood seasoning and stir. Add remaining onion, celery and bell pepper. Raise the heat to high and cook until the celery is tender, about 5 minutes. Add the garlic, bay leaf, 1 teaspoon of the seafood seasoning and the Tabasco sauce. Keep

stirring. The mixture will start sticking to the bottom. Deglaze with the remaining 1 cup of white wine and let reduce until almost dry.
- Add the tomatoes and cook over medium heat stirring and scrapping the bottom, for about 10 minutes. Add remaining seasoning, stock, tomato sauce and sugar. Reduce the heat to a simmer.
- Heat another sauté pan over high heat. Add olive oil and butter, and sauté seasoned shrimp. Cook the shrimp several at a time being careful not to over-crowd the pan. Sear them for about 40 seconds per side.
- Drain the shrimp on a rack or on paper towels. Continue cooking until all the shrimp are cooked, then add the shrimp to the sauce mixture, and cook until shrimp are tender and pink. Serve immediately on Cajon rice or black pepper pasta.

Vegetables

Vegetables add color, texture, flavor, and nutrients to your meals. They also pose certain challenges. For instance, if you cover the vegetables while cooking, they will discolor. Their flavor and consistency changes substantially as they cook as well. Vegetables that are cooked properly will have vibrant color and a lot of flavor. Green vegetables contain chlorophyll which gives them the green color and most of their flavor. There are several factors that affect the texture and color of the vegetable at the end of the cooking process. Acids, like citrus juice or zest, vinegar, or wine, have a firming effect on vegetables, and can lengthen the cooking time slightly. Alkalines are present in water and baking soda and will break down a vegetable making it soft and reducing the natural nutrients. So, vegetables that are cooked for shorter amounts of time contain more of their natural nutrients and vegetables that are over-cooked become mushy and lose their flavor and texture, which does not add to the appeal of your recipe.

Type	Pigment	Effects from Acids	Effects from Alkalines
Green Vegetables: Asparagus, Broccoli, Green Beans, Peas, Green Leafy Vegetables	Chlorophyll	Greens turn to a khaki green color.	The green color is vibrant and natural.
Yellow and Orange Vegetables: Bell pepper, Carrots, Rutabaga and Tomatoes	Carotenoids	No change.	No change.
Red, Purple and Blue Vegetables: Eggplant, Radishes, Red Leafy Vegetables	Anthocyanins	Reds are brightened.	Blues are brought out.
Vegetables that are Yellow White: Cauliflower, Potatoes, Onions, and Garlic	Anthoxanthins	Whites are brightened.	Yellows are more pronounced.

Methods for Cooking Vegetables

Dry Heat Cooking Methods

This includes grilling, baking, roasting and sautéing. Dry heat cooking methods will bring out the natural sugars and will intensify the flavor of the vegetables. Dry heat evaporates the water content of the vegetable, which is why the flavor intensifies.

Grilling

Grilling uses dry high heat and adds color, caramelizes the sugars in the vegetable and adds a smoky flavor. Grilling works well with vegetables that cook relatively quickly or vegetables that have been previously blanched. Mushrooms, onions, eggplant and peppers are good examples of vegetables that cook relatively quickly. Many times I have blanched green beans or asparagus and then finished them on the grill. Grilled asparagus with a little lemon juice, olive oil, salt and pepper is really nice.

Baking or Roasting

Baking or roasting is a dry heat method that softens and intensifies the flavor of vegetables. As a vegetable roasts, the water content evaporates, the flavor intensifies and the natural sugars become very prevalent. This is a good method for cooking hard vegetables such as carrots, potatoes, garlic, and squash. Roasting tomatoes, eggplants, onions, shallots and garlic really intensifies their flavor and sweetness.

Sautéing

Sautéing, which means to jump in the pan, involves high heat and a little fat or oil. This technique works well with blanched vegetables such as green beans and asparagus as a finishing process. Sautéing also works well with high moisture vegetables such as tomatoes, zucchini, and yellow squashes. Use this technique when you want to brown, add color, or add a caramelized flavor to your vegetables.

Moist Heat Cooking Methods

Moist heat cooking methods include blanching, braising, poaching and stewing.

Blanching

Blanching is the process of exposing vegetables to boiling water or steam for a brief period of time. Blanched vegetables will have better color and flavor than unblanched vegetables and the brief heating reduces the number of microorganisms on food and enhances the color of green vegetables.

To blanch your vegetables, drop them into boiling water until their color brightens and they soften slightly. This usually takes 2 to 3 minutes. When you remove them from the boiling water, drop them into an ice bath (a bowl of water and ice). The cold water will shock the vegetables and stop them from cooking any further.

Vegetables can be blanched ahead of time, placed in the refrigerator, and sautéed just before serving. Try sautéing in butter or flavored oil and shallots. Many other things can be added, such as nuts, fresh or dried herbs and many types of citrus. Experiment and find the flavor combinations that work for you!

Braising

Braising is the name we associate with cooking in liquid in a covered pot or Dutch oven. The amount of liquid used should be enough to reach the top of the ingredient being braised. Most often braising is done in the oven for longer periods of time and begins at 180°. Because of the longer cooking time, it is better to leave vegetables in larger pieces when braising. Also, select your braising liquid carefully, because the vegetables will pick up the flavor of the braising liquid.

Poaching

Poaching is often associated with chicken, fish, or eggs and is done to keep the foods moist. The food is completely immersed in liquid at a temperature just below the boiling point. The liquid is brought to a boil, the food is placed in the boiling liquid, the heat is reduced so that the liquid is at a gentle simmer, and the pan is covered. Water is often used as the poaching liquid, but other ingredients can be added to the water to provide additional flavor. Chopped aromatic vegetables such as carrots, onions, and celery can be added to the water as well as herbs and spices. No additional fat is adding during poaching, making it a healthy cooking method.

Stewing

Stewing is a moist cooking method similar to poaching, but with stewing the food is only partially immersed in liquid and then covered with a lid. Both methods can be used on the stovetop or in the oven.

Vegetable Recipes

Bruschetta

Ingredients:

6 to 8	Roma Tomatoes (depending on size)
1 Medium	Shallot or 1 Small Red Onion
6 to 8 Large	Basil Leaves
Splash	Good Quality Olive Oil
Splash	Balsamic Vinegar or Red Wine Vinegar
To Taste	Salt and Pepper
1	French Baguette
	Parmesan Cheese, grated for garnish

Method:

- Mix all ingredients except the bread and Parmesan cheese and let macerate ½ hour.
- Taste and adjust seasonings.
- Slice bread on the diagonal and brush with some olive oil. Toast until golden.
- Top bread with the tomato mixture and fresh shaved Parmesan cheese and serve.

Chipotles in Adobo Sauce

Chipotles in adobo sauce are Jalapeños that have been smoked and then stewed in a lightly seasoned liquid. They have become very popular in Southwestern cooking because they provide a distinctive, warm heat and delicious smoky flavor. They can be added to almost anything, including breads, sauces, salad dressings and pastas.

Ingredients:
- 7 to 10 Medium .... Dried, smoked, Jalapeño Chilies (Chipotles), stemmed and slit lengthwise
- 1/3 Cup .... White Onion, cut into ½" slices
- 5 Tbsp .... Cider Vinegar
- 2 Cloves .... Garlic, sliced
- 4 Tbsp .... Ketchup
- 1 Tsp .... Mexican Oregano
- ¼ Tsp .... Salt
- 1½ Cups .... Water
- 1½ Cups .... Chicken Stock

Method:
- Combine all of the ingredients in a pan. Partially cover and cook over very low heat for 1 to 1½ hours, until the chilies are very soft and the liquid has been reduced to 1 cup.
- This recipe will keep for several weeks in the refrigerator in an airtight container.
- For chipotle puree, place the cooked chipotles and sauce in a blender and puree. Put through a fine sieve to remove the seeds. Makes 1 cup.

Green Beans and Butternut Squash

Ingredients:

¾ to 1 Lb	Fresh Green Beans
1 Small to Med	Butternut Squash, peeled and cut into small cubes
1 Tbsp	Butter
1 Tbsp	Shallots, finely chopped
To Taste	Salt and Pepper
1 Tbsp.	Dried Basil
4 to 5 Tbsp.	Damson Plum Jelly or Jam

Method:

- Blanch the green beans and butternut squash until al dente (an Italian term meaning "to the tooth" which means to cook something enough to be firm but not soft) and place in an ice bath to stop the cooking.
- Heat a pan over medium-high heat; add the butter, shallots, salt, pepper, basil, and the Damson plum jam.
- Let the ingredients cook together until they form a sauce.
- Add the green beans and the butternut squash and cook until the vegetables are warmed through.
- If the sauce reduces too much, add a little water or chicken stock.

Green Beans with Pecans and Bread Crumbs

Ingredients:

½ Lb	Green Beans, trimmed and washed
2 Tbsp	Butter
¼ to ½ Cup	Pecans, chopped
1 Tbsp	Breadcrumbs
To Taste	Salt and Fresh Ground Pepper

Method:

- Fill a large pot with salted water and bring to a boil. While the water is coming to a boil, prepare an ice bath for the green beans. The ice bath is used to shock the vegetables and stop the cooking process of the green beans.
- As the water comes to a boil, reduce the heat to a simmer; place the green beans in the pot, and let cook 3 to 5 minutes, or to the desired doneness.
- Remove the green beans from the pot and immediately place them in the ice bath to stop the cooking process.
- Heat a sauté pan over medium-high heat. Make sure you let the pan heat completely before adding anything to it. This should take about 5 minutes.
- Place 2 tablespoons of butter in the pan and heat until slightly brown. Add the chopped pecans and the breadcrumbs, toss to coat, and cook until fragrant.
- Drain the green beans and toss into the butter, pecan, and breadcrumb mixture. Let cook until the green beans have warmed through. Taste the green beans and add salt and pepper to suit your taste.

Grilled Asparagus with Butter and Lemon

Ingredients:

3 to 4 Tbsp	Butter
1 Tbsp	Olive Oil
Zest of 1	Lemon
Juice of 1	Lemon
1 Clove	Garlic, minced
To Taste	Salt and Pepper
1 Bunch	Fresh Asparagus

Method:
- Place a 2-quart sauce pan over medium heat. Add the butter and cook until melted. Add the oil, lemon zest, lemon juice, garlic, salt and pepper.
- Wash the asparagus and pat dry. Place the asparagus on a sheet pan and coat with half the sauce, turning to coat.
- Pre-heat the grill to medium-high heat. Place the asparagus on the grill and cook for 5 to 6 minutes or until al dente.
- Remove from the grill, place in a serving bowl, and pour the remaining sauce on top to serve.

Grilled Eggplant Roll-ups

Ingredients:

4	Asian Eggplants
	Olive oil
To Taste	Salt and Pepper
1 or 2	Red Peppers, for roasting
2 Pkgs.	Goat Cheese or Cream Cheese
1 Pkg.	Fresh Basil
	Fresh Parsley or Dill, for garnish

Method:

- Wash the eggplant and slice lengthwise ¼" thick.
- Lightly coat the eggplant with olive oil and season with salt and pepper.
- Pre-heat or grill or pan. While the grill or pan is heating up, roast the red peppers. This can be done on a grill, right on the spider grate on your gas stove-top, or under the broiler. The goal is to blacken the skin of the pepper on all sides. After the skin is blackened, place the pepper(s) in a bowl and cover with plastic wrap to let cool. This process will help loosen the skin. When the pepper is cool enough to handle, peel off the blackened skin and discard.
- Grill the eggplant over medium-high heat, just long enough for some nice grill marks to form (about 2 to 3 minutes per side). After grilling, place on a tray to prepare them for rolling.
- To create the rolls, place a small strip of roasted red pepper (cut about 1" x 2") on each eggplant strip, followed by a good smear of goat cheese, and top with a basil leaf.
- Roll the eggplant up and garnish with fresh parsley or a sprig of dill.

Mushroom Stuffed Crepes

Ingredients:

2 Tsp	Olive Oil
3 Tbsp	Butter
¾ Lb.	Mushrooms, sliced (use any one kind you like or a combination)
Pinch	Salt and Pepper
1 Small	Shallot, finely chopped
1 Clove	Garlic, finely chopped
¼ Cup	Cognac
1 Cup	Veal or Chicken Glaze
1 Tsp	Tarragon or Thyme
1 Recipe	Crepes (See recipe in 'Pastry and Dessert Recipes' section of the book.)
1 Recipe	Red Wine Pan Sauce (See recipe in 'Sauce Recipes' section of the book.)
	Sour Cream (optional)
	Fresh Parsley, for garnish

Method:

- Heat a sauté pan over medium-high heat and add the oil and butter to the pan and let cook about two minutes, until the butter smells nutty.
- Slice the mushrooms into bite-sized pieces and add them to the pan in batches. You want the mushrooms to caramelize slightly and, if they are all added at once, the mushrooms will release their moisture and they will boil. Season with salt and pepper.
- Remove each batch of mushrooms and set aside when all done.
- Add a little more olive oil, add the shallots, and cook until softened.
- Add the garlic and cook one minute. Deglaze with the cognac and reduce by half.
- Add the veal or chicken stock and reduce until thickened. Add the tarragon and the cooked mushrooms. Cook until warmed through and then swirl in the last remaining butter.
- To make the crepes, layout a crepe on a plate, fill half the crepe with 2 to 3 tablespoons of the mushroom filling. Fold over the crepe, and drizzle some red wine sauce on top. You can also add a dollop of sour cream and garnish with fresh parsley.

Spicy Slaw Salad

Ingredients:
- 35% .... Jicama
- 35% .... Chayote
- 10% .... Carrots
- 20% .... Granny Smith Apples
- 2 Tsp. .... Rice Wine Vinegar
- ¾ Tsp. .... Habañero, finely minced
- 1 Tsp. .... Serrano Chiles, finely minced
- 1 Tsp. .... Sugar
- Juice of ½ .... Lime
- Zest from ½ .... Lime
- To Taste .... Salt

Method:
- Shred or finely julienne the jicama, chayote, carrots, and apples and mix in the proportions listed.
- Combine the rest of the ingredients and toss with the slaw.
- Let sit in the refrigerator for at least 30 minutes and serve

Tubers

A whole book could be written on tubers alone. Tubers are used throughout the world, from Asia and Africa, to Mexico and the United States. They each have a unique flavor and can be cooked in many ways. Tubers can be boiled, broiled, fried, roasted, steamed, and grilled to name a few. Below is a partial list of the tubers that are familiar to me.

Potatoes

Potatoes are probably the most well known of the tuber family. They are starchy and hardy and can be cooked like a vegetable, made into flour, processed for chips or even used for distillation mash!

There are many different types of potatoes available at the market today. Potatoes are categorized by the amount of starch they contain. As to which one is best to use, it really comes down to the flavor and texture you are trying to achieve. Listed below are some general guidelines for the different types of potatoes and some guidelines for their best uses.

We have all heard of new potatoes, which are young potatoes the have not been allowed to fully mature. They are usually young red or white potatoes. New potatoes have thin skins, a slightly waxy texture, a lower amount of starch, and higher moisture and sugar content then other types of potatoes. I generally boil, sauté, or roast new potatoes. They are also great for potato salad.

Some types of potatoes are also referred to as old potatoes. Old potatoes include Idaho, russet, and Burbank. Old potatoes have a thicker skin, a higher starch content, and lower sugar and moisture content than new or medium potatoes. These are potatoes that lend themselves to stuffing. Old potatoes are also ideal for French fries and baking. When these types of potatoes are fried, baked or boiled, they produce a fluffier result then all other potatoes because of the high starch content. Also, when you want really fluffy mashed potatoes, boil the potatoes whole with the skins left on. Leaving the skins on the potato will limit the amount water that is absorbed during the cooking process resulting in a creamier end product. And remember, when boiling potatoes, always start with cold water and salt the water.

There are several other types of potatoes referred to as medium potatoes. Medium potatoes are categorized as chefs white, white rose, blue, fingerlings and Yukon gold. Their starch, sugar and moisture content lie somewhere between the old and new potatoes listed above. The medium starch potatoes will work with all methods of cooking.

Potatoes do require care when storing. Make sure they are kept in a cool, dark, dry place – preferably in a brown paper or burlap bag with holes in it. Ideally, the temperature should remain steady at about 50° to 60° F. And don't store them in the refrigerator, or they will become too sweet. You can store them for up to a month or two if they are mature. You shouldn't store new potatoes for more than a week. And avoid the temptation to store them with your onions (which like a lot of the same conditions.) When close together, onions and potatoes produce gasses that spoil each other.

Boniato and Sweet Potatoes

Boniato, also known as the Cuban sweet potato, is mealy and has white flesh, unlike the sweet potato. Sweet potatoes have an orange colored skin and yellow or orange flesh. Both are cooked the same - they can be boiled, steamed, fried, roasted or grilled.

Red sweet potatoes and boniato are fairly high in sugars and lend themselves well to cooking on the grill, as the sugars caramelize and give the end product a great flavor.

Yams are not sweet potatoes as many think. They are a tuber, however, and are indigenous to Asia and Africa. Yams can grow up to 8 pounds, are not as sweet or moist as sweet potatoes, and can be cooked just like a sweet potato or boniato.

Jicama

Jicama is a relative of the potato and is widely popular in Asia, Latin America, and Mexico. Jicama looks like a turnip or a very large radish and has a thin brown skin. Jicama can be used in many ways - from adding crispness to salads to being cooked with other vegetables. It has a crunchy texture and tastes similar to apple or pear; in fact it goes well with both and Jicama will not turn brown when exposed to the air like apples or pears. In the Vegetables section of this book I have created a salad using Jicama that is wonderfully crispy and crunchy. When Jicama is cooked, it has a tendency to take on the flavors of the vegetables or meat that it is cooked with and is great for adding to stir-fry dishes. When purchasing, look for blemish free skin, a dry root and a firm texture. Jicama can be stored for up to two weeks in a plastic bag in the refrigerator.

Parsnips

Parsnips are cold-weather root vegetables. They are related to carrots, are easy to prepare and are a healthy stand-in for potatoes with many meals. Parsnips are also a nice addition to soups and stews.

They resemble an off-white carrot and have a mild celery-like fragrance and a sweet, nutty flavor. Unlike carrots, parsnips contain no beta-carotene but they are a good source of vitamin C. Their flavor is best in winter when they are most abundant. Although they can grow up to 20" long, they are most tender when they are about the size of a large carrot. To store them, keep them in a perforated plastic bag in the refrigerator crisper. They should last for three to four weeks.

Parsnips are almost always eaten cooked, as they tend to be quite fibrous. Some typical ways of cooking them include roasting, mashing, glazing, creaming, or dicing them up and adding them to soups and stews.

Sunchokes

Sunchokes are a relative of the sunflower and are native to America. Although their names are similar, sunchokes are not related to the artichoke. The flesh is white and crunchy when served raw. When cooked in theirs skins, they become more like potatoes, but have a nutty flavor, and a mild taste of artichoke. These would be another good substitute for potato. Choose sunchokes that are firm and free from molds and wrinkles. They can be stored in a plastic bag in the refrigerator for up to one week.

Taro Root

Taro root is another good substitute for potatoes. Taro is widely known in the Polynesian Islands and probably best known as Poi, which is mashed taro root. Taro root has a hairy skin, much like a coconut. Taro must be cooked before eating, as it is toxic in its raw form and the outer skin is always removed from the taro root and cannot be eaten. Always wear plastic or rubber gloves when peeling the taro, as the juice that is extracted can cause irritations to the skin. My favorite way to eat taro root is to clean and slice it very thin and fry it to make taro root chips. They go great with sandwiches! Simply fry the chips at 350° to 360° until crisp, then drain and enjoy!

Water Chestnuts

Water chestnuts, looks similar to chestnuts, but are from Southeast Asia. They are the roots of an aquatic plant that grows in fresh water. Water chestnuts are delightfully crunchy and are a great addition to any dish when you want to add texture. Finding fresh water chestnuts is not easy, however. More than likely you will be using canned water chestnuts, which are fine but be sure to drain them and rinse with water before using. Always dry the water chestnuts before adding to a stir-fry. A good Asian Grocery can be a source for fresh water chestnuts. And if you are interested in becoming a better Asian cook, get to know your Asian grocer as you would get to know your butcher. They know their products and can tell you the best ones to use for each purpose. When you are lucky enough to find fresh water chestnuts, look for nuts that are firm and have no wrinkles and make sure you peel them before cooking with them or eating them.

Yucca

Yucca is a white and starchy tropical vegetable. It has a firmer flesh than potatoes as well as a higher starch content. Yucca has a dark brown skin that looks a lot like tree bark.

You store yucca as you would potatoes or freeze tightly wrapped for up to a month. Yucca is a good substitute for potatoes - they can be boiled and then mashed with milk, cream, butter, salt and pepper. When buying yucca, look for tubers that are blemish free.

Potato and Other Tuber Recipes

Layered Potato Casserole

Ingredients:

1 Tbsp.	Butter
2	Potatoes, cleaned and thinly sliced
¼ Cup	Chicken Stock
1 Pint	Cremini Mushrooms, thinly sliced
1¼ Cups	Cheddar Cheese, grated
2-3 Tbsp.	Fresh Rosemary, chopped
To Taste	Freshly Ground Pepper
6-8 Tbsp.	Cream
2-3 Tbsp.	Fresh Marjoram, chopped
1¼ Cups	Havarti Cheese, grated
¼ Cup	Dried Bread Crumbs

Method:

- Coat the bottom and sides of a rectangular casserole dish with the butter. Line the bottom of the pan with half of the potato slices, overlapping them slightly.
- Drizzle the potatoes with half of the chicken stock. Place half the mushrooms on top of the potato slices and then sprinkle on half the cheddar cheese. Top this with the rosemary and some freshly ground pepper. Drizzle with half the cream.
- Now create a second layer. Lay out the remainder of the potatoes, overlapping them slightly. Then drizzle with the remainder of the stock and top that with the remaining mushrooms and cheddar cheese. Sprinkle with the marjoram and some freshly ground pepper. Drizzle with the remainder of the cream, and then sprinkle on the Havarti cheese and the breadcrumbs.
- Bake in a 350° oven for about an hour or until the potatoes are tender and the cheese and breadcrumbs on the top are golden brown.

Variations on a Theme:

There are numerous ways to make this recipe your own. It was actually begun as an idea as a friend and I were wandering through the grocery store trying to decide what to make for dinner. We came up with the basic concept and bought a few items. Once we started putting the dish together, it was pure creativity. The technique is all about layering. You can change any of the layers. Use sweet potatoes instead of russets. Change the type of mushrooms. Don't use mushrooms. Do a meat layer with bacon, or pancetta, or chicken. Instead of a side dish, it could become an entrée. Change the herbs. We chose rosemary and marjoram partly because they were growing fresh in my herb garden at the time. Choose the herbs you like best or that you think will complement the rest of the meal. Altering the stock you use will change the nature of the dish as well. So will changing the type of cheese you use. Imagine the dish with some jalapeño-jack cheese. The key here is to go with your instincts as to what flavors will blend well and then give it a try. You'll never know how terrific a dish can be until you actually put it to the test. Dare to step outside the safety zone of your trusty cookbook and try something new!

Mashed Potatoes

Ingredients:

3 Medium............Baking or Idaho Potatoes, washed
4 Tbsp. ....Butter
¾ Cup..................Heavy Cream
To Taste ....Salt and Pepper

Method:
- Fill a 6-quart pan about 2/3 full of water and place it on a burner over high heat. Place the unpeeled potatoes in the pan and cook until the potatoes are tender, about 25 minutes.
- Drain the water and peel the potatoes (if desired). Then add the butter and cream and mash them to a smooth consistency. Add salt and pepper to taste and serve.

Variations on a Theme:
- Try adding ¾ cup of Parmesan cheese and 1 tablespoon of freshly chopped thyme.
- Try adding 6 ounces of goat cheese and 2 tablespoons of fresh thyme.
- Try adding any cheese and herb combination that tickles your fancy. Some of the other things I like to add are: caramelized onions or a couple of cloves of roasted garlic.

Tip: I always make extra mashed potatoes because, when I was a child, my Mom used to make potato cakes in the morning. They are so delicious and easy to make. Simply take some of your leftover mashed potatoes and form them into a patty like a hamburger. Coat the flat sides with flour. Heat a sauté pan over medium-high heat, place a little butter, bacon grease, or best of all a little duck fat in the pan and add the potato cake when the oil is hot. Cook until golden brown, about 3 to 5 minutes on a side. Serve with a couple slices of crispy bacon and a slice of toast.

Potato cakes are also great with steak, fried chicken or even pan seared pork chops with caramelized onion gravy.

French Fried Potatoes

(Serves 2 as a meal portion or 3-4 as an appetizer portion)

Ingredients:
2 .... Potatoes, cleaned and sliced as described below
.... Oil, for frying – can use vegetable, peanut, safflower, canola, etc.
To Taste .... Salt and/or Pepper

Method:
- Wash and peel the potatoes (for boardwalk style fries, leave the skins on). Slice the ends and sides off to form a rectangle. Slice the potatoes into sticks that are roughly ¼" x ¼" x the length of the potato, or Alumette 1/8"x 1/8"x 2½". This will take less time if you have a mandolin or V-slicer.
- Place the sliced potatoes in a large bowl and cover with cold water. Place in the refrigerator for at least one hour or as long as 6 hours. This will remove excess starch from the potatoes.
- After soaking, drain and place the potatoes on a sheet pan lined with paper towels and pat them dry with additional paper towels.
- Heat up your deep fryer to 325°. If you do not have a deep fryer, use a 4 to 6 quart Dutch oven and fill 1/3 full with oil. Remember, the oil will expand when the potatoes are added and the last thing you want is to have oil boil over onto your stove, so don't overfill the pot.
- Cook the potatoes in small batches (adding too many will drop the temperature of the oil too much) until they are a very pale yellow. Remove each batch from the oil and drain on a wire rack. Don't drain them on paper towels or the potatoes may soak up the excess oil. At this point the potatoes will be mostly cooked on the inside. Cook the remaining potatoes and place on the wire rack.
- Place in the refrigerator 1 hour, several hours or overnight.
- Pre-heat the oven to 300°. Heat the oil in your deep fryer or Dutch oven to 375°. Cook the fries in small batches until golden brown, drain on wire rack. Season each batch of the fries with salt, pepper or your favorite seasoning. Place in the oven to keep warm while cooking the rest of the fries.

Oven Roasted Parsnip Puree

<u>Ingredients:</u>

6	Parsnips, peeled and cut into 1" sections
1 Tbsp.	Olive Oil
To Taste	Salt and Pepper
¾ to 1 Cup	Heavy Cream, Half and Half, or Whole Milk (the heavy cream will have the richest taste)
1 Tsp	Thyme

<u>Method:</u>

- Pre-heat the oven to 350°. While the oven is pre-heating, peel and cut the parsnips. Place in a bowl, pour the olive oil in the bowl, and toss to coat. Sprinkle with salt and pepper to taste.
- Pour the parsnips onto a sheet pan and place in the oven. Roast them for 30 to 40 minutes or until golden brown and soft on the inside.
- Place into a 4-quart pan and smash using a potato masher. Pour in the cream and the thyme and whip with a whisk or hand mixer.

Tip: This is nice served with roast chicken, roast pork or roast beef.

Oven Roasted Potatoes

Ingredients:
3 Medium .... Baking or Idaho Potatoes, peeled and cut into 1" pieces
3 Tbsp. .... Olive Oil
2 Tbsp. .... Rosemary, finely chopped
To Taste .... Salt and Pepper

Method:
- Pre-heat the oven to 350°. While the oven is pre-heating, peel and cut the potatoes.
- Place the potatoes in a bowl, pour the olive oil over them, and toss to coat. Sprinkle with the fresh rosemary and add salt and pepper to taste while tossing in the bowl to coat evenly.
- Pour the potatoes onto a sheet pan and place in the oven. Roast for 30 to 40 minutes or until golden brown and soft on the inside.

Tip: This is nice served with roasted chicken, roast pork or roast beef.

Oven Roasted Root Vegetables

Ingredients:

1 Medium	Sweet Potato, peeled and cut into 1" pieces
4	Parsnips, peeled and cut into 1" pieces
2	Turnips, peeled and cut into 1" pieces
3 Tbsp.	Olive Oil
1 Tsp. each	Fresh Thyme and Rosemary, finely chopped
To Taste	Salt and Pepper

Method:

- Pre-heat the oven to 350°.
- Place in a bowl, pour the olive oil in the bowl, and toss to coat. Sprinkle with the fresh herbs and add salt and pepper to taste, tossing in the bowl to coat evenly.
- Pour the root vegetables onto a sheet pan and place in the oven. Roast them for 30 to 40 minutes or until golden brown and soft on the inside.

Tip: This is nice to serve with roasted chicken, roast pork or roast beef.

Soy Grilled Sweet Potatoes

(Enough marinade for up to 2 pounds of sweet potatoes)

Ingredients:

2 lbs .... Sweet Potatoes, Yams or Boniato

Marinade

¼ Cup .... Soy Sauce
1 Tbsp. .... Rice Vinegar
1 Tbsp. .... Ginger, minced
2 Cloves .... Garlic, minced
2 Tbsp .... Olive Oil
1 Tsp. .... Sesame Oil

Method:

- Put the sweet potatoes (whole, UNPEELED, potatoes) in a large saucepan with enough water to cover them. Bring the water to a boil and cook until the potatoes are just tender, about 25 to 30 minutes. Using unpeeled potatoes keeps them from absorbing too much water and makes the resulting potato fluffier.
- Drain and rinse the potatoes under cool water. Cut them into ½" thick slices and arrange them in a dish.
- Combine all the marinade ingredients and pour the marinade over the potatoes. Marinate for 30 minutes.
- Prepare a hot fire. Cook the potatoes on the grill for 1 to 2 minutes, turn them, brush with more marinade and cook for another minute or two, until the potatoes are browned and glossy. Enjoy!

Pizza

In my quest for the perfect crust, I think I must have tried every pizza dough recipe on the planet. Bread flour, all purpose flour, and cake flour are just a few of the flours I have tried. In the resulting pizza dough listed in this book, you will see I use 00 Flour. You may have some difficulty finding 00 Flour, but I promise you, it's worth the trouble.

After the flour, the second most important contributor to the success of your pizza is your oven. If you have a gas oven, invest in a pizza stone. Having a stone in the oven helps hold in the heat, so when you're opening and closing the door, it helps the oven stay hot. The stone is placed in the bottom of the oven and, for convenience; I leave mine in the oven all the time and only remove it when I clean the oven. If you have an electric oven, the best thing is to place your stone on a rack in the lowest position.

Heat is important. Pre-heat the oven for at least 15 to 20 minutes to bring the oven and the stone up to temperature. When your oven is ready, place the pizza directly on the stone.

As the pizza cooks, check the crust for doneness. You can do this by inserting the peel under the pizza or using a metal spatula. The crust should be nice and brown and crisp. I also like the cheese to be well browned. If the pizza crust is ready and the cheese is not, move the pizza from the stone and place it on the highest rack in your oven. Since heat rises, the top will cook and be browned within a minute or two, but the crust should not continue to brown significantly.

Pizza Recipes

Neapolitan Pizza Dough

(Makes 4 – 10" to 12" Pizza Crusts)

Ingredients:

1½ Cups	Water
1 Tsp	Dry Active Yeast
1 Tsp	Honey
4 Cups	00 Ground Flour (available at La Cuisine in Old Town Alexandria, VA. If you do not have 00 Ground Flour, you can get pretty close by using 3 cups of all purpose flour and 1 cup of cake flour.)
1 Tbsp	Kosher Salt
	Corn Meal for the Pizza Peel

Method:

- Fill a 2 cup measuring cup with 1½ cups of water. The water should be warm, 95 to 100°. Dissolve the yeast and the honey in the water and stir to incorporate. Let the mixture proof 5 to 10 minutes, or until foamy.
- While the yeast mixture is proofing, add the flour to a stand up mixer bowl and place the dough hook on the mixer. With the mixer on slow speed, add the salt to the flour and mix to combine for 1 minute. As the mixer is turning, slowly add the water and yeast mixture. Knead the dough for 30 minutes on low speed. After 30 minutes, remove the dough from the bowl and form into a ball.
- Place in a lightly oiled bowl, turning to coat the ball of dough. Cover and let rise in the bowl for a minimum of 4 hours. The longer and slower the rise of the dough, the better it will taste. Often I make the dough the day before and let it rise in the refrigerator with plastic wrap tucked around the dough to keep it from drying out.
- After 4 hours, remove the dough from the bowl. Punch the dough down and divide the dough into 4 equal parts. Shape the divided dough into balls. Place on a sheet tray, cover and let rise an additional 2 hours.
- Pre-heat the oven to 500° with a pizza stone in the oven. If you have a gas fired oven, place the pizza stone on the floor of the oven. If you have an electric oven, place the pizza stone on the lowest rack position. I leave mine at the bottom of my oven all the time. This will also help hold the heat in the oven.
- Now the fun starts. To form the crust, place the dough onto a lightly floured work surface. Flatten the ball of dough from the center out with your fingertips. Grab the dough near the edge and rotate the round and stretch the dough as you rotate. If you are feeling a little adventurous, you can try to toss the pizza dough in the air. This takes some practice, but it's quite impressive as your guests watch.
- Stretch the dough into a 10" to 12" round. For a thinner crust it can be stretched to 14". Take your pizza peel out and sprinkle with some corn meal. The corn meal is used to keep the pizza dough from sticking to the peel and making it easier to slide onto the stone.
- If you don't have a peel, you can remove the stone from the oven, sprinkle on some corn meal, and make the pizza directly on your stone. Just be careful handling it when it's hot.
- Use this recipe as the foundation for any of your favorite pizzas.

Pizza Sauce

Ingredients:

1 to 2 Tbsp.	Olive Oil
1 Tbsp.	Red Onion, minced
1 Clove	Garlic, minced
1 - 28 oz. Can	Good Quality Italian Whole Tomatoes
1 Tbsp.	Basil, Thyme, Oregano or Marjoram (it's really a matter of taste)
1 Tsp.	Red Pepper Flakes (optional or more if you like the sauce spicy)
1 Tbsp.	Non-flavored Tomato Paste
To Taste	Salt and Pepper

Method:

- Heat the olive oil in a 3-quart pot over medium-high heat. Add the onions and sauté until tender. Add the garlic and cook, being careful not to burn it.
- Crush the tomatoes with your hands, pour into the heated pot, and bring to a slow simmer. Taste and adjust the seasonings.
- Add the remaining ingredients and cook for 30 to 40 minutes until slightly thickened. Taste again and adjust the seasonings.
- Insert an emulsion blender (boat motor) into the sauce and blend into a smooth consistency.

Tip: I usually double or triple this recipe and freeze the leftover sauce for the next time I make pizza.

Pizza Margarite

Ingredients:
1 Recipe .... Neapolitan Pizza Dough
1 Recipe .... Pizza Sauce
.... Fresh Buffalo Mozzarella Cheese
.... Fresh Basil

Method:
- Place the tomato sauce on the pizza, being careful not to add too much. If too much sauce is added, you run the risk of your cheese sliding off.
- Add the fresh buffalo mozzarella cheese slices and fresh basil and slide into the oven. In a 500° oven it will take 4 to 5 minutes for the bottom to become crispy. If you like the cheese a little browned on top, place on the uppermost rack for 1 to 2 minutes more.

Pasta

The pasta recipe in this book is a basic pasta recipe and can be used to create many different types of pasta. This recipe can be used for making lasagna, fettuccini, linguine, and ravioli, just to name a few. There are many things you can add to pasta to change the flavor and color. In the case of spinach pasta, spinach is obviously added. The spinach is cooked before adding it to the pasta to soften the leaves and make them more flexible. Frozen spinach that has been thawed, also works very well. The important thing to remember is that, prior to adding it to the pasta; you need to ring out as much water as possible. This would hold true for anything moist that you add to the pasta, such as tomatoes. The more moisture you add, the more flour you must use to soak up the additional moisture.

Basic Pasta

Ingredients:
1 Cup .... All Purpose Flour
1 .... Egg
1 Tbsp. .... Olive Oil
Good Pinch .... Salt

Method:
- This recipe will make a meal portion for two or an appetizer portion for 4. Increase the ingredients based on the number of people you are serving.
- Place the flour on a cutting board and make a well in the center. Add the egg, olive oil and salt. With a fork, beat the egg like you are making scrambled eggs, slowly incorporating the flour into the egg mixture. Always pull a little flour at a time into the center. If you have leftover flour, don't worry. You may not need all the flour you start with. Continue mixing until the pasta forms into a thick paste, then knead the pasta until it forms a soft ball.
- Starting with the pasta machine on the widest setting, roll the pasta through the machine. If the pasta is a bit sticky add some of the reserved flour. Continue this process until the pasta is smooth and elastic. Now start running the pasta through the narrower settings on the machine until you reach the desired thickness.

Sun-Dried Tomato and Balsamic Pasta Salad

Ingredients:

1 – 1 Lb. Box	Penne Pasta, cooked al dente
20	Basil Leaves, cut into fine julienne
1 – 8.5 oz. Jar	Sun-Dried Tomatoes Packed in Olive Oil, drained
½ Lb.	Fresh Whole Milk Mozzarella Cheese, cut into small cubes

Vinaigrette

½ Lb.	Fresh Whole Milk Mozzarella Cheese, cut into small cubes
½ Cup	Balsamic Vinegar
2 Cloves	Garlic, finely chopped
2 Small	Shallots, finely chopped
2 Tbsp	Country Grain Dijon Mustard
To Taste	Salt and Pepper
¾ Cup	Olive Oil

Method:

- Place all the ingredients for the vinaigrette, except the olive oil, into a blender. Blend the ingredients, and then slowly drizzle in the olive oil to make the vinaigrette.
- Place the pasta in a large bowl with the sun-dried tomatoes and most of the basil. (Reserve a little basil for the top).
- Toss to combine. Add half the vinaigrette and toss to combine. Add more of the vinaigrette if needed.
- Top with the reserved, finely chopped basil.

Variations on a Theme:

Also try adding some shaved Parmesan cheese or Pecorino cheese. This is really nice with some grilled chicken and grilled corn on the cob.

A Little Something on the Side

Fried Rice

(Serves 3 to 6)

Fried rice is something you can have a lot of fun with and add your own style to. You can add garlic, stir-fried chicken, beef, pork or ham. Try using pork, shrimp and chicken for a triple delight. I have done mushroom fried rice with a nice selection of wild mushrooms. Don't be afraid to experiment!

One of the biggest secrets to a good stir-fry is the mis en place. Remember, this is French for 'everything in its place'. In other words, have all of your ingredients cut and prepared to go into the wok before you heat it up.

Ingredients:

6 oz.	Chinese Sausage
1/3 Cup	Green Onions, finely chopped
3 or 4	Eggs
2 Tsp + 1 Tbsp	Vegetable Oil
3 Cups	Cooked White Rice (brown rice can also be used)
1 Tbsp	Soy Sauce
¼ Tsp	Salt
¼ Tsp	White Pepper
1 Cup	Frozen Peas, thawed

Method:

- Cut the Chinese sausage in half lengthwise and then cut it into ¼" slices on the diagonal. Place the slices in a small bowl. Slice the green onions and reserve.
- Lightly beat the eggs.
- Heat a pan over medium-high heat for a couple of minutes. Add 2 teaspoons of oil and swirl the oil into the pan to coat the sides. Add the sausage and cook for about 2 minutes, until slightly crispy. Remove and reserve.
- Add the eggs and cook about one minute. As soon as the eggs start to set, lightly break them up with a stabbing motion.
- Add the remaining oil and swirl. Add the rice and slowly add the soy sauce, salt and pepper. Stir-fry for about 2 to 3 minutes breaking up the rice to separate and to evenly coat the rice.
- Add the peas and continue to cook for 2 to 3 minutes or until the rice begins to slightly brown.
- Add the sausage and scallions and continue to cook one minute or until well combined. Serve piping hot for "wok hay'. Wok hay is a term used to describe the elusive taste imparted to food fresh from a wok that only lasts a minute or two. This is why it is served piping hot.

Grandma's Hush Puppies

Ingredients:

1 Cup	White Corn Meal
½ Cup	All-Purpose Flour, sifted
2 Tsp.	Baking Powder
½ Tsp. Each	Salt and Pepper
2	Eggs, beaten
1 Tsp.	Onion, grated
1 Clove	Garlic, minced
¾ to 1 Cup	Milk
	Enough Oil to Cover the Hush Puppies

Method:

- Mix corn meal, flour, baking powder, salt and pepper in a bowl. Add the beaten eggs, onion, and garlic, and enough milk to make a stiff batter. Cover the bowl and place it in the refrigerator until the batter becomes spongy.
- Heat the oil to 375°. Drop the batter by spoonfuls into the hot oil and fry until golden brown, approximately 4 to 5 minutes. Drain on absorbent paper.
- Serve with fried fish, fried chicken or by themselves as a snack.

Variations on a Theme:

Try cooking your favorite sausage or smoked chopped beef, chicken or pork and stuffing the hush puppies. Dip into barbeque sauce or your favorite dipping sauce.

Rice Pilaf with Dried Cranberries and Toasted Pine Nuts

(Serves 3 to 6)

Ingredients:

1 Tsp.	Olive Oil
1 Small	Shallot, finely chopped
2 Cups	Long Grain Jasmine White Rice
¼ Cup	White Wine
¼ Tsp	Salt
½ Cup	Toasted Pine Nuts
½ Cup	Dried Cranberries, chopped

Method:

- Place a 4-quart pot over medium-high heat. Add the olive and the shallots and cook 2 to 3 minutes.
- Stir in the rice to coat and cook until the rice has turned opaque white.
- Add the wine, and let cook 1 minute.
- Add 2½ cups of water and ¼ teaspoon of salt. Cover and cook 12 minutes. Do not uncover.
- Turn the heat off and continue to cook another 3 minutes.
- Uncover and stir in the toasted pine nuts and the cranberries.

Tip: A nice way to serve this is to pack a small bowl (½ to 1 cup size) with rice. Hold the cup in one hand and place a plate on top. Turn the plate over, while holding the bowl in place. When the plate is turned over, remove the bowl. The rice will remain in the shape of the bowl. Arrange the rest of the main course around the rice.

Pastries and Desserts

Pastries and desserts are relatively simple and a lot of fun to make. But keep in mind that baking is a much more scientific endeavor than savory cooking and the recipes are more exacting.

The best pastry recipes are written using weight measurements rather than volume measurements, since weight is more exact. Instead of calling for a cup of flour, a recipe might call for 5 oz. of flour. Flour is especially susceptible to moisture in the air and, depending on a number of factors, 1 cup of flour might weigh anywhere from 4 to 6 ounces! This explains why many people get inconsistent results when they bake. As a good rule of thumb, weight measures are preferred when baking.

There are basically 2 types of pastry - sweet and savory. The technique for each is very similar, but sweet pastry is, of course, sweet, and savory pastry is not.

As you will notice, most of the recipes in this book that use pastry are based on Pate Sucree. This is a traditional French pastry that I learned at school and it makes a great foundation for many pastry recipes.

As with all cooking, making pastry involves a series of techniques. I myself still have much to learn about pastries and look forward to continuing my education in this area. In the meantime, I have focused my efforts in the book around what I know best, so most of the desserts included in this section are built around fruit.

Pastry and Dessert Recipes

Basic Crepes

Ingredients:
7 oz.	All Purpose Flour
Pinch	Salt
1	Egg
1 oz	Butter, melted

Sweet Crepes
3 Tbsp	Sugar
1 Tbsp	Your Favorite Liqueur

Method:
- Combine the flour and salt (and sugar if making sweet crepes) into a bowl. Add the egg and the butter and mix to combine. If the mixture is too stiff, add just enough milk to combine. While mixing, add the remaining milk to create a smooth batter. My mom always used a large spoon and beat the mixture like eggs until smooth. The mixture must be free of lumps. Place the batter in the refrigerator for 1 hour.
- Heat a crepe pan over medium heat and brush a light coat of butter in the pan. Add a ladle of the batter to the pan and swirl the crepe pan to coat. Crepes should be very thin. Cook until golden brown and flip the crepe to cook the other side.
- Stuff or fold the crepe to suit the dish you are making. If serving later, place on a plate and keep warm in the oven.

Variations on a Theme:
For savory crepes try using fresh herbs in the mixture. I do crepes stuffed with mushrooms. In the crepe batter I have either thyme or tarragon. For sweet crepes, try adding some of your favorite liqueurs, such as amoretto, coffee, chocolate, or mint.

Caramel Sauce

Ingredients:
Equal Parts........... Sugar and Cream
.... Water

Method:
- Place sugar in a heavy saucepot (something non-reactive like stainless steel) and add enough water to moisten the sugar to a "wet sand" consistency. (Don't worry if you add too much, it will still work, it will just take longer.)
- Heat over high heat, but don't stir it. If absolutely necessary, you can swirl the pan, but don't stir. As the sugar cooks, there will be lots of small bubbles and as it continues to cook, the bubbles will become much larger. This is a sign that the caramel is getting closer to being finished
- Cook until the caramel has a nice deep reddish brown color. Be very careful not to burn it. It goes very quickly from close to done to burnt.
- Pour the cream in. When you do, it will bubble up. Stir it. It will "seize" or harden. Don't panic. Keep it on the heat and keep stirring. It will all smooth out and become a nice, creamy caramel sauce.
- Pour into a squirt bottle and store in the refrigerator.

Chocolate Mango Ravioli

<u>Ingredients:</u>
1 Recipe .... Crème Anglais (See recipe in this section of the book.)

Pasta
1 Cup – 6 Tbsp ..... All Purpose Flour, sifted
3 Tbsp .... Cocoa Powder
3 Tbsp .... Confectioner's Sugar
1 Large .... Egg
1 Tbsp .... Butter, melted
Pinch .... Salt

Filling
1 Tbsp .... Butter
2 .... Mangos, one chopped into small cubes, one whole
1 Tbsp .... Brown Sugar
¼ Tsp .... Cardamom
1/8 Tsp .... Cinnamon

<u>Method:</u>
For the Filling:
- Peel the mango and cut into ¾" pieces. In a medium sauce pan melt the butter over medium heat. Add the chopped mango, brown sugar, cardamom and cinnamon and cook until well blended and broken down. Let cool.

For the Ravioli:
- You have replaced 6 tablespoons of flour with 3 tablespoons of cocoa and 3 tablespoons of confectioner's sugar. Otherwise, this recipe for pasta is made just like the recipe in the 'Pasta' section of the book.
- After the pasta reaches the desired thickness, roll it out and fill each ravioli with one tsp of the mango puree and a chunk or two of the raw mango.
- Cook in boiling water until al dente maybe 6-8 minutes. Remove from the water and drain on a rack until cool.
- Cut leftover pasta into fettuccini strips and boil until cooked.

To Serve Coat the plate with Crème Anglais and arrange 2-3 raviolis in it. Take the fettuccini strips and create nests around the ravioli and add chunks of mango to the top of each nest. For added color top with kiwi or strawberry.

Coconut Sorbet
(Serves 4)

Ingredients:
2/3 Cup .... Sugar
6 Tbsp. .... Water
2 Tbsp. .... Dark Rum
1 - 15 oz. Can .... Coconut Milk

Method:
- Place the sugar in a 3-quart saucepan and add the water and rum. Bring to a boil and remove from the heat. Cool in an ice bath.
- Add the coconut milk and stir to incorporate. Place mixture in the refrigerator to cool for 1 hour or until cold.
- Add the mixture to an ice cream maker and process following the manufacturer's directions or until frozen.
- If you do not have an ice cream maker, place in a 9 x 12 baking dish and freeze, scraping and stirring with a spoon every ½ hour until light and smooth.

Crème Anglais

<u>Ingredients:</u>

1½ Cups .... Heavy Cream
3 .... Egg Yolks
1/3 Cup .... Sugar
½ Tsp .... Almond Extract
¼ Tsp .... Vanilla Extract

<u>Method:</u>

- Heat the heavy cream over low heat and let cook until small bubbles start to form around the outside of the pan.
- While the cream is heating, beat the egg yolks in a clean stainless steel bowl and add the sugar and beat until pale yellow. Add the extracts to the egg yolk mixture to combine.
- While whisking, slowly add some of the cream to temper the egg yolk mixture. Do not add all at once, or you might scramble the eggs. Slowly add a little at a time until the mixture has reached the same temperature as the cream. Once this happens, stir the egg mixture back into the remaining cream, stirring with a wooden spoon. Slowly heat the cream and egg mixture until it has thickened enough to coat the back of the spoon. Remove from the heat and let cool.
- Add a piece of plastic wrap on top of the Crème Anglais to keep a skin from forming. When ready to use, transfer into a squeeze bottle.

Crepes with Caramelized Sugar and Orange Butter Sauce

Ingredients:

¼ Cup .... Sugar
½ Cup .... Cream
¼ Cup .... Orange Liquor
Zest of 1 .... Orange
4 Tbsp .... Butter
1 Recipe .... Crepes (see crepe recipe from above)

Method:

- Place the sugar in a 2-quart sauce pan and add enough water to moisten the sugar. (Don't worry if you add too much, it will still work, it will just take longer.)
- Heat over high heat, but don't stir it. If absolutely necessary, you can swirl the pan, but don't stir. As the sugar cooks, there will lots of small bubbles and as it continues to cook, the bubbles will become much larger. This is a sign that the caramel is getting closer to being finished.
- Cook until it is a nice deep reddish brown color. Be very careful not to burn it. It goes very quickly from close to done to burned.
- Pour cream into the mixture and it will bubble up. Stir it. It will "seize" or harden. Don't panic. Keep it on the heat and keep stirring. It will all smooth out and become a nice, creamy caramel sauce.
- Add the orange liquor and orange zest and cook 2 minutes, remove from the heat and stir in the butter.
- To prepare, fold the crepes into quarters and drizzle with the sauce.

Dark Chocolate Truffles

(Makes about 75 1/3 oz. Truffles)

Ingredients:

7 oz.	Heavy Cream
½ Tsp	Vanilla, Almond, or Hazelnut Extract
1 lb	High Quality Dark Chocolate, finely chopped
2 oz.	Butter, melted
	Coating (Dutch Processed Cocoa Powder or Chopped Nuts or Coconut, or Mexican Cinnamon)

Method:

- Heat the cream and vanilla or other flavoring to a simmer.
- Chop the chocolate and place it in a bowl. When the cream is at the simmer, pour the cream over the chocolate and stir until the chocolate is completely melted. Let cool slightly.
- When cooled, add the butter and stir to incorporate, then place the mixture in the refrigerator and let cool for several minutes.
- What you have now is called 'Chocolate Ganache'.
- When the mixture has cooled again, scoop out about 2 teaspoons at a time and roll into balls. Place in the refrigerator until firm.
- Finish by rolling the balls in the coating of your choice.

Empanadas Pastry

Ingredients:

2 Cups	All Purpose Flour
½ Tsp	Salt
½ Cup	Water
1 Tbsp	Sugar
1	Egg Yolk, beaten
¼ Cup	Butter or margarine, melted
1	Egg White, lightly beaten
	Lard or Oil, for deep frying

Method:

- Sift the flour and salt into a bowl.
- Mix together the water, sugar and egg yolk. Make a well in the center of the flour and pour the liquid mixture into the well.
- Slowly mix together until a dough forms.
- Bend and knead the dough until smooth. Leave to rest for 15 minutes.
- Roll out half the pastry very thinly on a lightly floured board and brush with half the melted butter. Roll up the pastry to a long, thin roll, making sure it is rolled tightly and firmly. Cut into slices about 2.5 cm (1") thick and roll each slice out to a circle about the size of a small saucer.
- Put a spoonful of filling on each saucer shaped pastry, brush the edges of the pastry with lightly beaten egg white, fold to a half circle shape and press edges firmly together to seal. Decorate the edge by using a fork. Repeat with the remaining pastry and fillings.
- Heat up the oil or the lard in a deep fat fryer or frying pan and, when it is moderately hot, fry the empanadas. Fry them a few at a time, until golden brown. Place them on an absorbent paper to drain the excess oil and serve warm.

Grilled Pineapple

Ingredients:

1 .... Pineapple, whole and fresh
½ Cup .... Honey
2 Tbsp. .... Cherry Brandy

Method:
- Prepare a medium fire.
- Remove the rind from the pineapple and slice into ½" to ¾" slices.
- Mix the honey and the cherry brandy together and brush it onto the pineapple slices. Grill for approximately 10 minutes, basting while cooking.
- Serve with coconut sorbet.

Leche Flan

Ingredients:

- 1 Cup .... Sugar
- 1/8 Cup .... Water
- 1 Cup .... Sweetened Condensed Milk
- 2½ Cups .... Evaporated Milk or 2 Cups Evaporated Milk & 1 Cup Whole Milk
- 20 Medium .... Egg Yolks
- 3 Drops .... Vanilla Extract
- Zest of 1 .... Lemon or Orange

Method:

- Make the caramelized sugar mixture first. In a 2-quart sauce pan over medium-high heat, add the sugar and the water. As the sugar dissolves, small bubbles will start to form and as it gets closer to the end of cooking, larger bubbles will form. Be careful not to over-cook. The color will change from light amber to dark amber. As the sugar reaches that dark amber color, remove the pan from the heat and pour into the baking dishes.
- In a large bowl, mix the condensed milk, evaporated milk, egg yolks, and vanilla extract. Mix with a wooden spoon until well incorporated.
- Strain it as you pour it into the dishes prepared with the caramelized sugar. Top the mixture with lemon or orange zest.
- Prepare a steamer and heat the water to a boil. Lower the heat to a low boil and place the dish inside the steamer and cover. Steam until set, about 30 minutes.

Pate Sucree

<u>Ingredients:</u>

8 Tbsp	Butter, softened (1 stick)
4 oz	Sugar
1	Egg
¼ Tsp	Vanilla or Almond Extract, or your favorite flavoring
Pinch	Salt
12 oz	All Purpose Flour

<u>Method:</u>

- Place the softened butter in a stand up mixer with the paddle attachment. Turn mixer on to low speed and mix the butter for 1 minute.
- Slowly add the sugar and mix to combine, about 1 minute.
- Add the egg and mix until completely incorporated. Add the vanilla, or other flavoring and a pinch of salt.
- Slowly add the flour. Mix the dough until it starts to come together and form small pebbles. Place a piece of plastic wrap on a flat surface, empty the dough onto the plastic wrap and form into a flat tight disc. Place in the refrigerator for at least 2 hours to rest.
- After the dough has rested, remove from the refrigerator for 10 minutes. Lay out a 12" x 12" sheet of plastic wrap on a flat surface, place the dough on the plastic wrap, and place another sheet of plastic on top. Roll out the dough turning it in 1/8 turns after each passing of the rolling pin. This will ensure the dough to be round. Roll out to about 1/8" thick and place it in a tart pan with a removable bottom.
- Place the tart pan on a sheet tray. Cut a circle of parchment paper and place it in the tart pan, then add dry beans to cover the paper. This will weigh down the dough and keep it from bubbling up and forming air pockets on the bottom of your tart.
- Place in a 350° oven and cook for about 12 to 15 minutes to set. Remove the beans and parchment paper and return to the oven for another 5 minutes. This process of baking the shell with no fillings is called blind baking.

Tips: This tart shell is the basic foundation for different flavored tarts. Now that you have the foundation, you can have a little fun with the fillings. Here are a few of my favorites:

- Wash some fresh blueberries and pick through them to remove any stems or bad berries. Add your cleaned blueberries to your tart shell then pour some caramel sauce (see recipe in this section) onto the blueberries, about ½ to ¾ cup. Place into a 350° oven and bake until the blueberries start to pop. About 30 minutes.
- Start with fresh granny smith apples that have been washed and peeled. Core the apples and quarter them, then slice them lengthwise into ¼" slices. Place the slices into a bowl as you go, squeezing a little lemon juice periodically to keep

the apples from turning brown. When you have finished slicing the apples, place them in your tart shell in a circle pattern overlapping the slices all the around the pan. Continue laying apples in an overlapping fashion until the tart is completely covered. Cover with caramel sauce (see recipe in this section), about ½ to ¾ quarter cup, sprinkle with ¾ cups of chopped pecans and bake in a 350° oven for about 30 minutes or until the apples are soft. To serve drizzle chocolate on the plate, place a slice on top of the chocolate and top with a scoop of vanilla ice cream.

- Make a batch of chocolate ganache (See the Dark Chocolate Truffle recipe in this section of the book.). Toast chopped hazel nuts, and let cool. Fill your blind baked 10" tart shell with the chocolate ganache topped with the toasted hazelnuts and ½ cup of caramel sauce. (See recipe in this section of the book.) Place in the refrigerator for at least 1 hour.

Peach Sunrise
(Serves 6)

Ingredients:
½ Cup	Sugar
2 Cups	White Wine
3	Ripe Peaches, peeled, cut in half, and pit removed
1 Recipe	Chocolate Ganache (See Dark Chocolate Truffle recipe in this section of the book.)
1 Recipe	Crème Anglais (See recipe in this section of the book.)
1 Recipe	Raspberry Coulis (See recipe in this section of the book.)

Method:
- Combine the sugar and white wine in a pan. Place the pan over medium heat and cook until the sugar dissolves.
- While the wine syrup comes to a simmer, peel, and cut the peaches in half. Once the peaches have been cut in half, remove the pits and, with a sharp pairing knife, enlarge the pit hole enough to hold a tablespoon of the chocolate ganache.
- Place the peach halves in the wine syrup and simmer until tender, about 15 to 20 minutes. Remove from the heat and let cool.
- To assemble the dessert, scoop about 1 tablespoon of chocolate ganache into the peach pit hole. If you have a scoop that lets you form a nice round ball with the ganache, all the better. Ladle a thin layer of Crème Anglais onto a plate. Place the peach, cut side down (hiding the chocolate), into the Crème Anglais. Squeeze a circle of raspberry coulis about an 1/8" thick around the peach. Drag a knife tip through the raspberry coulis out from the peach and through the Crème Anglais to give the look of a sunburst.

Raspberry Coulis

<u>Ingredients:</u>

½ Cup................... Sugar
½ Cup................... Water
2 Pints .... Fresh Raspberries, discard any discolored or bad raspberries

<u>Method:</u>
- Combine the sugar and the water in a medium pan and bring to a low boil. Cook until the sugar has dissolved. This is called a simple syrup.
- Add the raspberries to the mixture and cook over medium-low heat until the raspberries break down and start to form a syrupy consistency.
- Pour through a fine mesh strainer and let cool. Transfer to a squeeze bottle.

Techniques

Removing Corn from the Cob

The best tool for this job is a sharp knife. If you want whole kernels, first cook the corn. This sets the milk in the corn and keeps the moisture in the kernels and not all over you. You can blanch the ears or roast them. Once the corn cools, stand the cob on its end in a shallow dish or small bowl and cut down the ear, removing a few rows at a time. A general rule of thumb is that one cob will yield about ½ cup of corn. If you just want the juicy pulp from the kernels, but not the skins, draw the tip of a knife down the center of each row to split the kernels open. Then, using the back of the knife, scrape down the cob to squeeze all the pulp and juices out of the skins. Be careful not to apply too much pressure or you'll pull the skins off the cob as well. The juice or "milk" you net from this process is wonderful in sauces, soups and dressings.

Keeping the Corn Together

The best tool for this is a bunt pan. Place an ear of corn (stalk side down) in the hole in the middle of the bundt pan. Cut the kernels off as described above. As you cut the corn, it will fall into the bundt pan. This will keep it from falling all over the counter.

Cutting Bell Peppers

The best way to cut a bell pepper is to stand the pepper up with the stem facing up. Slice the pepper about half an inch from the stalk down lengthwise from top to bottom. Turn ¼ turn and slice again. Continue until all four sides have been cut off. When finished, the stalk and the bulb with the seed will be intact. When slicing the peppers into strips, always cut with the skin side down, as it is much easier to cut through. The white veins are bitter, so trim this part from the quartered peppers and discard.

Removing the Heat from Chilies

When using chilies to cook for guests that shy away from spicy-hot foods, make sure all the white veins and seeds have been removed from the chiles. Much of the heat is in the veins and seeds. Also, roasting the chilies will tone down some of the heat.

Roasting Bell Peppers and Chilies

There are several methods for roasting bell peppers and chilies, but the method I use most often is directly on the spider grates of my gas stove. To do this, simply turn your burner on and place the bell pepper directly on the grate, letting the gas flame char the outside skin of the pepper. As the pepper chars, rotate it to get even coverage and continue until all sides are blackened. When ready, place the pepper in a large bowl and cover tightly with plastic wrap. This will cause the pepper to steam, making it easy to remove the skin. In fact, the plastic wrap may even fog up and expand slightly forming a dome on top of the bowl. Let the pepper steam until it is cool enough to handle and then gently remove the skin and discard. What you have left is a nicely roasted pepper. When using this method for chilies, place a small grate over the burner and follow the same method.

A second method is to use the broiler in your oven. For this method, start by slicing the pepper into quarter's lengthwise and placing the quarters on a sheet tray, skin side up. Place the tray under the broiler and cook until the skin is blackened. Watch closely as you only want the skin to char, not the meat of the pepper. When the peppers are charred, remove and place in a large bowl and cover tightly with plastic wrap. When cool enough to handle, gently remove the skin and discard.

You can also do this on your outdoor gas or charcoal grill. Follow the same method as described above, just use your grill as the heat source.

Making Flavored Olive Oils

Instead of buying expensive oils, consider making them. They are very easy to make.

For one cup of flavored olive oil, place a medium pan on the stove. Place the olive oil in the cold pan. Add ½ cup of fresh herbs to the oil and heat over medium-low heat for 5 to 8 minutes. Remove from the heat and let cool. Strain in a fine mesh strainer and place in a bottle. Store in the refrigerator.

Glossary

00 Flour

In Italy, flour is classified either as 1, 0, or 00, which refers to how finely ground the flour is and how much of the bran and germ have been removed. Doppio zero is the most highly refined and is talcum-powder soft. This is available from La Cuisine in Alexandria, Virginia. See their website at www. lacuisineus.com

Blanch

Blanching is the act of dipping food into boiling water for a short time, then dipping immediately in cold water and draining. Blanching is done to partially cook vegetables for later use or to loosen skins on nuts or fruits like almonds, tomatoes and peaches. After being dipped in the boiling water, skins can be easily slipped off. Blanching also destroys enzymes and sets the colors in vegetables that are to be frozen.

Boil

To boil is to cook food in a boiling liquid. Julia Child defines seven stages of heating water in her book From Julia Child's Kitchen. Other chefs have their own definitions, but most are similar to these.

1. **Tepid**: 85° to 105°.
2. **Warm**: 115° to 120°.
3. **Hot**: 130° to 135°.
4. **Poach**: 180° to 190°. Julia Child calls this stage a "shiver", because it is the point when the water starts to move.
5. **Simmer**: 190° to 200°. At this stage, bubbles begin to appear in the water.
6. **Slow boil**: 205°. Slow rising bubbles begin to form at this stage.
7. **The full or rolling boil**: 212°. During this stage, bubbles break the surface.

Bouquet Garni

A bunch of herbs that are loose or tied together in cheesecloth and used to flavor soups, stews and broths. Putting the herbs in the cheesecloth makes it easy to remove them before the dish is served. Typically a bouquet garni consists of bay leaves, whole black pepper corns, fresh parsley and thyme.

Caramelize

Caramelize literally means to convert or change into caramel. This technique of sautéing food to bring out the sugars and brown the outside is used frequently with onions, shallots, and fennel.

Chiffonade

In French this literally means "made of rags." In cooking, it refers to thin strips or shreds of vegetables or herbs (usually basil or lettuce).

Chop

Chopping involves cutting ingredients into small pieces. Chopping results in irregular sized and shaped pieces that are slightly larger than a dice.

Clarified Butter

Also called 'drawn butter', it is butter that has been heated, evaporating most of the water and separating the milk solids (which sink to the bottom of the pan) from the golden liquid on the surface. After the removal of the solids, what remains is clarified butter. Because the milk solids have been removed, clarified butter has a higher smoke point than regular butter, so it can be used for cooking at higher temperatures.

Crème Fraiche

A matured, thickened cream with a slightly tangy, nutty flavor and velvety rich texture. Crème fraîche is ideal for adding to sauces or soups because it can be boiled without curdling.

Deglaze

Deglazing is the act of adding liquid to a pan to loosen and dissolve the brown bits and pan drippings that formed during cooking and basting. To deglaze a pan, first remove the food and excess fat from the pan. Then, add a liquid, such as stock, water, wine, brandy, etc. and heat, scraping the browned bits from the bottom of the pan. Deglazing is often the basis for making sauces.

Demi-Glaze

A "half glaze" made by slowly cooking veal stock until it's reduced by half to a thick glaze that coats a spoon. This intense flavor is used as a base for many other sauces.

Dice

Dicing is the act of cutting food into small, regular sized cubes. A dice is usually a cube-shaped cut measuring about 1/8" to ¼" in size. A dice is larger than a mince, but smaller than a chop.

Emulsion

A mixture of two liquids which normally don't combine smoothly - oil and water being the classic example. Emulsifying is done by slowly adding one ingredient to another while mixing very quickly. This disperses and suspends minute droplets of one liquid throughout the other.

Ice Bath

A bowl filled with ice and water used to 'shock' blanched, boiled or steamed vegetables and stop the cooking process.

Macerate

To make something soft by soaking it in a liquid. In cooking, this usually means to soak fruit in a liquid (usually a liqueur) in order to infuse it with the liquid's flavor.

Marinate

To soak food in a seasoned liquid mixture to transfer the flavors of the mixture or 'marinade'.

Mince

Mincing creates very small pieces of food. A mince is much smaller and finer than a dice.

Mirepoix

A mixture of carrots, onions, celery and herbs used to season sauces, soups, stocks, and stews.

Mis en Place

A French term for having all the ingredients necessary for a dish gathered together in advance of cooking.

Parboil

Parboiling is partially cooking a food by boiling it for a short time in water. Dense foods like carrots and potatoes are often parboiled and then added near the end of a recipe so that all the ingredients finish cooking at about the same time. When parboiling, the food may continue to cook after being removed from the boiling water. Just as with blanching, you should refresh it in an ice water bath to stop the cooking process and set the color.

Pizza Peel

A flat, smooth, shovel-like tool used to slide pizzas and yeast breads in and out of the oven and onto a baking stone.

Purée

To grind or smash food until it's totally smooth. You can use a food processor or blender or you can force the food through a sieve.

Reduce

Reducing is the act of condensing a liquid by applying heat. As the water in the liquid evaporates, the remaining ingredients become more concentrated and thick. Reducing liquids intensifies their flavor. Reduction is a common process when working with stocks and making sauces.

Roasting

To roast meat, poultry or vegetables is to cook them, uncovered, by dry heat (usually in an oven). The cooking is done at a high temperature and creates a browned, crispy surface and seals in the natural juices.

Roux

A roux is a mixture of flour and melted fat (butter, olive oil, etc.) that is cooked until it reaches a desired color and texture. It is then used to thicken soups and sauces.

Sauté

To sauté is to cook food quickly over high heat in a skillet or sauté pan. A small amount of fat or oil is used and it must be very hot before the food is added so that it will cook quickly, brown the outside, and seal in the natural juices in the food. Do not crowd the pan or add too much food too quickly. Doing this lowers the temperature of the pan and results in steamed or soggy food, rather than sautéed. The word sauté comes from the French verb meaning "to jump".

Sear

Searing browns the surface of a food. This is done quickly over very high heat and can be done in a skillet, under a broiler, on a grill, or in the oven. The purpose of searing is to seal in natural juices and create a crispy exterior. Searing is often done to help seal in a food's juices prior to braising or roasting.

Simmer

Simmering is cooking liquid or a food in liquid over medium heat just below the boiling point. When simmering, small bubbles are just beginning to rise to the surface which occurs at about 190° to 200°.

Sweat

To sweat is to soften vegetables by cooking in a very small amount of fat over gentle heat so they release their juices into the fat but do not turn brown. This concentrates the juices in the cooking fat.

Zest

The colored outer portion of the peel on a piece of citrus fruit. It does not include the white pith which is bitter.

International Conversion Chart

The recipes in this book are all measured in American amounts. The American and some of the Canadian pints are 16 ounces. The British, Australian, and some Canadian recipes use the Imperial pint which is 20 fluid ounces. The American tablespoon is 14.2 ml; the Australian Tablespoon is 20ml; the British Tablespoon is 17.7ml; and the Canadian Tablespoon is 15ml. This can be confusing, so be careful when converting recipes from other countries. This is especially true for pastry recipes.

American	European
1/8 teaspoon	½ ml
¼ teaspoon	1 ml
½ teaspoon	3 ml
1 teaspoon	5 ml
1 Tablespoon	15 ml
1/8 cup	35 ml
¼ cup	65 ml
½ cup	125 ml
¾ cup	190 ml
1 cup	250 ml
½ ounce	15 g
1 ounce	30 g
¼ pound	115 g
½ pound	225 g
¾ pound	340 g
1 pound	464 g

Oven Temperature Chart

160 degree Fahrenheit =	70 degree Celsius
200 degree Fahrenheit =	100 degree Celsius
250 degree Fahrenheit =	120 degree Celsius
300 degree Fahrenheit =	150 degree Celsius
350 degree Fahrenheit =	180 degree Celsius
400 degree Fahrenheit =	200 degree Celsius
450 degree Fahrenheit =	230 degree Celsius
500 degree Fahrenheit =	260 degree Celsius
Broil =	Grill

Index

Alfredo Sauce, 30

Barbecue Sauce, 31
  Mustard Based, 32
  Tomato Based, 33
  Vinegar Based, 34
Basic Crepes, 172
Basic Pasta, 164
Béchamel, 22
beef
  Carne Asada, 80
  Hungarian Goulash, 81
  Mechado ala Marie-A Typical Filipino Dish, 83
  Negimaki, 84
  New Shepherds Pie, 85
  Smoked Brisket, 95
  Smoked Stuffed Tomatoes, 99
Beef Brisket Rub, 12
Beef Stock, 17–18
Bills Shrimp and Feta over Spaghetti Squash, 123
Blackberry Pan Sauce, 34
boniato. *See* tubers
Brandy Veal Stock Reduction, 35
Bruschetta, 138

Cajun Empanadas, 78
Caramel Sauce, 173
Carne Asada, 80
Champagne Soup with Smoked Chicken, 51
chicken
  brine, 110–111
  Citrus Marinated Chicken, 112
  cutting, 103–109
  General Tso's Chicken, 113
  Pan-Seared Chicken and Wild Mushrooms, 114
  Smoked Chicken, 96
  Szechwan Chicken, 118
  Tequila Chicken, 119
Chicken Stock, 19
Chipotles in Adobo Sauce, 139
Chipotle Tomato Salsa, 36
Chocolate Mango Ravioli, 174
Citrus Marinated Chicken, 112
Coconut Sorbet, 175
conversion chart, international, 193
cooking techniques, 186–187
Crawfish Egg Rolls, 124
Crawfish Etouffee, 125
Cream of Mushroom Soup, 52

Creole Seafood Seasoning, 12
Crème Anglais, 176
Crepes with Caramelized Sugar and Orange Butter Sauce, 177

Dark Chocolate Truffles, 178
desserts. *See* pastries and desserts
duck
  Roast Duck Asian Style, 116–117
  Smoked Duck Breast, 97
  Tea-Smoked Duck, 102

Empanadas Pastry, 179
Espagnole (Basic Brown Sauce), 23

Fish Stock, 20
French Fried Potatoes, 153
Fried Rice, 9, 167

Garlic and Mushroom Butter Cream Sauce, 37
General Tso's Chicken, 113
glossary, 188–192
Grandma's Hush Puppies, 168
Green Beans & Butternut Squash, 140
Green Beans with Pecans and Bread Crumbs, 141
Green Chili Soup, 5, 53
Grilled Asparagus with Butter and Lemon, 142
Grilled Eggplant Roll-ups, 143
Grilled Fish Tacos, 126
Grilled Pineapple, 180

Hearty Beer & Cheese Soup, 54
Herb Crusted Rock Fish with Sauce Beurre Blanc, 127
Hollandaise, 24
Hungarian Goulash, 6, 81

Jamaican Seasoning, 13
jicama. *See* tubers

knife skills, 62–71
  construction of knives, 63
  culinary cuts, basic, 68–70
    chiffonade/shredding, 69
    of onions and shallots, 69–70
    other cuts, 70
  decorative cuts, 70–71
    fluting, 71
    tourne, 70–71
  garlic paste, 71

  holding the knife, 68
  production of knives, 64
  purchasing knives, 65
  sharpening and steeling, 67
  steel, method for using, 68
  types of knives and their uses, 65–67
  wet stone, method for using, 68

lamb
  Lamb Kabobs, 90
  Merguez Kefta, 91
  Rack of Lamb Stuffed with Brandy Macerated Apricots, 92
Lamb Kabobs, 90
Layered Potato Casserole, 151
Leche Flan, 181
Lemon Veal Glaze Sauce, 38
Lime Butter Sauce, 39

Mango Salsa, 40
Mashed Potatoes, 152
Meatloaf for Sandwiches, 82
Mechado ala Marie-A Typical Filipino Dish, 83
Merguez Kefta, 91
Mother Sauces, 21, 22
Mushroom Stuffed Crepes, 144

Neapolitan Pizza Dough, 160
Negimaki, 84
New Shepherds Pie, 85

olive oils, flavored, 187
Osso Bucco, 86
Oven Roasted Parsnip Puree, 154
Oven Roasted Potatoes, 155
Oven Roasted Root Vegetables, 156
oven temperature chart, 193

Pan-Seared Chicken and Wild Mushrooms, 114
Pan Seared Duck Breast 7, 115
Pan Seared Steak, 5, 74
Pan-Seared White Fish, 8, 125
parsnips. *See* tubers
pasta, 163–165
  Basic Pasta, 164
  Sun-Dried Tomato and Balsamic Pasta Salad, 165
pastries and desserts, Dark Chocolate Truffles, 178
pastries and desserts, 170–185

Basic Crepes, 172
Caramel Sauce, 173
Chocolate Mango Ravioli, 174
Coconut Sorbet, 175
Crème Anglais, 176
Crepes with Caramelized Sugar and Orange Butter Sauce, 177
Empanadas Pastry, 179
Grilled Pineapple, 180
Leche Flan, 181
Pate Sucree, 182
Peach Sunrise, 184
Raspberry Coulis, 185
Pate Sucree, 182
Peach Sunrise, 10, 184
pizza, 8, 122, 158–162
  Neapolitan Pizza Dough, 160
  Pizza Margarite, 162
  Pizza Sauce, 161
Pizza Margarite, 162
Pizza Sauce, 161
Poached Salmon with Citrus Butter sauce, 130
pork
  Cajun Empanadas, 78
  Meatloaf for Sandwiches, 82
  Mechado ala Marie-A Typical Filipino Dish, 83
  Pork Chops with Caramelized Onion Pan Gravy, 87
  Sausages in Grape Sauce, 88
  Smoked Pork Tacos, 98
  Southwestern Smoked Stuffed Tomatoes, 100–101
Pork Chops with Caramelized Onion Pan Gravy, 87
potatoes. *See* tubers
Poultry Seasoning, 14

Rack of Lamb Stuffed with Brandy Macerated Apricots, 6, 92
Ras Al Hanout (Moroccan Spice), 14
Raspberry Coulis, 185
Red Wine Pan Sauce, 40
Rice Pilaf with Dried Cranberries and Toasted Pine Nuts, 169
Roast Duck Asian Style, 116–117
Roasted Acorn Squash Soup, 55
Roasted Chestnut Soup, 56
Roasted Corn and Chorizo Soup, 57
Roasted Corn Chowder, 58

sauces, 21–26
  Alfredo Sauce, 27
  Barbecue Sauce, 31
  Mustard Based, 32
  Tomato Based, 33
  Vinegar based, 34
  Blackberry Pan Sauce, 34

Brandy Veal Stock Reduction, 35
Caramel Sauce, 173
Chipotle Tomato Salsa, 36
Garlic and Mushroom Butter Cream Sauce, 37
Lemon Veal Glaze Sauce, 38
Lime Butter Sauce, 39
Mango Salsa, 40
Mother Sauces
  Béchamel, 22
  Espagnole (Basic Brown Sauce), 23
  Hollandaise, 24
  Velouté, 22
  Vinaigrette, 25–26
Red Wine Pan Sauce, 40
Simple Tomato Sauce, 41
Spirit Pan Sauce, 42
Tomatillo Salsa, 43
Tomato Concasse Sauce, 44
Tomato Vodka Sauce, 45
vinaigrette
  Champagne Vinaigrette, 28
  Rice Wine Vinaigrette, 28
Wild Mushroom Sauce, 46
Sausages in Grape Sauce, 88
seafood, 120–133
  Bills Shrimp and Feta over Spaghetti Squash, 123
  Crawfish Egg Rolls, 124
  Crawfish Etouffee, 125
  Grilled Fish Tacos, 126
  Herb Crusted Rock Fish with Sauce Beurre Blanc, 127
  Pan-Seared White Fish, 129
  Poached Salmon with Citrus Butter sauce, 130
  Seven Spice Shrimp and Mango Salsa, 131
  Shrimp Creole, 132–133
seasoning mixtures, 11–15
  Beef Brisket Rub, 12
  Creole Seafood Seasoning, 12
  Indian Seasoning, 13
  Jamaican Seasoning, 13
  Poultry Seasoning, 14
  Ras Al Hanout (Moroccan Spice), 14
  Southwestern Seasoning, 15
  Steak Seasoning, 15
seasoning mixtures
  Ras Al Hanout (Moroccan Spice), 14
  Steak Seasoning, 15
Seven Spice Shrimp and Mango Salsa, 131
Shrimp Creole, 132–133
Shrimp Stock, 20
side dishes, 166–169
  Fried Rice, 167
  Grandma's Hush Puppies, 168

Rice Pilaf with Dried Cranberries and Toasted Pine Nuts, 169
Simple Tomato Sauce, 9, 41
Smoked Brisket, 7, 95
Smoked Chicken, 96
Smoked Chicken Soup, 59
Smoked Duck Breast, 97
Smoked Pork Tacos, 98
Smoked Stuffed Tomatoes, 99
smoking, 93–102
  Smoked Brisket, 95
  Smoked Chicken, 96
  Smoked Duck Breast, 97
  Smoked Pork Tacos, 98
  Smoked Stuffed Tomatoes, 99
  Southwestern Smoked Stuffed Tomatoes, 100–101
  Tea-Smoked Duck, 102
soups, 50–61
  Champagne Soup with Smoked Chicken, 51
  clarified, 48
  Cream of Mushroom Soup, 52
  garnish for soups, 49
  Green Chili Soup, 53
  Hearty Beer & Cheese Soup, 54
  meats in soups, 48
  Roasted Acorn Squash Soup, 55
  Roasted Chestnut Soup, 56
  Roasted Corn and Chorizo Soup, 57
  Roasted Corn Chowder, 58
  Smoked Chicken Soup, 59
  Tortilla Soup, 60
  Tuscana Soup, 61
Southwestern Seasoning, 15
Southwestern Smoked Stuffed Tomatoes, 100–101
Soy Grilled Sweet Potatoes, 137
Spicy Slaw Salad, 145
Spirit Pan Sauce, 42
steak, 72–76
  buying, 72
  grilling, 74
  lamb, basic cuts, 75–76
  other cuts of beef, choosing, 75
  pan-seared and oven-roasted, 74
  prepping, 73
Steak Seasoning, 15
stocks, 16–20
  Beef Stock, 17–18
  Chicken Stock, 19
  Fish Stock, 20
  Shrimp Stock, 20
  Veal Stock, 18–19
  Vegetable Stock, 17–18
sunchokes. *See* tubers
Sun-Dried Tomato and Balsamic Pasta Salad, 165
sweet potatoes. *See* tubers

Szechwan Chicken, 118

taro root. *See* tubers
Tea-Smoked Duck, 102
Tequila Chicken, 119
Tomatillo Salsa, 43
Tomato Concasse Sauce, 44
Tomato Vodka Sauce, 45
Tortilla Soup, 60
tubers, 146–157
  boniato and sweet potatoes, 147
    Soy Grilled Sweet Potatoes, 137
  jicama, 147
  parsnips, 147
    Oven Roasted Parsnip Puree, 154
  potatoes, 146
    French Fried Potatoes, 153
    Layered Potato Casserole, 151
    Mashed Potatoes, 152
    Oven Roasted Potatoes, 155
  sunchokes, 148
  taro root, 148
    Oven Roasted Root Vegetables, 156
  water chestnuts, 148
  yucca, 149
Tuscana Soup, 61
Typical seasonings, 4

veal
  Meatloaf for Sandwiches, 82
  Osso Bucco, 86
Veal Stock, 18–19
vegetables, 134–145
  bell peppers, cutting, 187
  Bruschetta, 138
  chilies, cooking/cutting techniques, 187
  Chipotles in Adobo Sauce, 139
  cooking methods, 135–136
  corn, cooking techniques, 186
  Green Beans and Butternut Squash, 140
  Green Beans with Pecans and Bread Crumbs, 141
  green peppers, cooking/cutting techniques, 186–187
  Grilled Asparagus with Butter and Lemon, 142
  Grilled Eggplant Roll-ups, 143
  Mushroom Stuffed Crepes, 144
  Spicy Slaw Salad, 145
  Typical vegetable cuts, 10, 68, 69
vegetables, *see also* soups
Vegetable Stock, 17–18
Velouté, 22
Vinaigrette, 25–26
  Champagne Vinaigrette, 28
  Rice Wine Vinaigrette, 28

water chestnuts. *See* tubers
Wild Mushroom Sauce, 46

yucca. *See* tubers